WORKFORCE 2020

WORK AND WORKERS IN THE 21ST CENTURY

WORKFORCE 2020

WORK AND WORKERS IN THE 21ST CENTURY

Richard W. Judy
and
Carol D'Amico

With contributions by
Gary L. Geipel
Justin A. Heet
Donald K. Jonas
Alan Reynolds
William Styring III

Hudson Institute
Indianapolis, Indiana

Hudson Institute
Indianapolis, Indiana

$16.95
ISBN #1-55813-061-6
Copyright © 1997 Hudson Institute,Inc.
Fifth Printing, August 1999

Printed in the United States of America

This book may be ordered from:
Hudson Institute
Herman Kahn Center
P.O. Box 26-919
Indianapolis, Indiana 46226
(317) 545-1000
1-800-HUDSON-Ø

CONTENTS

ILLUSTRATIONS

Figures

Tables

ACKNOWLEDGMENTS

This book is dedicated to Roger Semerad, former U.S. Assistant Secretary of Labor, Hudson Trustee, and Executive Director of the Workforce Project, for without him this book would not have been possible. Our deepest appreciation to Roger, who supported us with his goodwill and enthusiasm throughout this project.

Workforce 2020 has had the benefit of counsel from a group of distinguished experts. An Advisory Committee met periodically to review, assist, and advise the research team on this study. The committee was chaired by Roger Semerad. It included William E. Brock, III, The Brock Offices and former U.S. Secretary of Labor; Anthony Carnevale, Vice President of Public Leadership, Educational Testing Service; Gary E. Doran, Vice President, Policy and Administration, AT&T Foundation; Steven H. Goldman, Director, Ball Foundation; Robert Guttman, Employment and Training Consultant and former U.S. Assistant Secretary of Labor; William B. Johnston, Executive Vice President, Burson-Marsteller; George A. Keyworth, II, Chairman, Progress & Freedom Foundation; Marie-Josée Kravis, Senior Fellow, Hudson Institute; Fred S. Lafer, President, Henry & Marilyn Taub Foundation; Stanley S. Litow, Vice President for Corporate Community Relations, IBM; Malcolm R. Lovell, President, National Planning Association; Rob Melnick, Director, Morrison Institute for Public Policy; Arnold Packer, Senior Fellow, Johns Hopkins University; Lawrence R. Phillips, Senior Human Resource Officer, Citicorp/Citibank; Esther Schaeffer, Consultant; and Ricky Silberman, Executive Director, Office of Compliance, United States Congress.

Many thanks to the following companies and organizations for their generous funding of this project: The Pew Charitable Trusts, American Express Foundation, AT&T, Automatic Data Processing, BP America, The Boeing Company, Chevron, Citicorp/Citibank, Delco Electronics, Ewing Marion Kauffman Foundation, General Hotels Corporation, Henry & Marilyn Taub Foundation, IBM, Merrill Lynch, The Walton Family Foundation, and a foundation that wishes to remain anonymous.

The research, writing, and analysis of *Workforce 2020* were left exclusively to the study's authors and do not necessarily reflect the views of these organizations.

Within the institute, many researchers and administrative staff made significant contributions to the study. We acknowledge the contributions of our editor, Joel Schwartz, who helped to make the complex issues understandable. We are also grateful to John Clark, Deborah Jones, Susan Protsman, Gwen Rosen, and John Weicher. We would also like to thank Hanneke Frese, David Murray, Jay Nordlinger, Tevi Troy, and William Wolfson. Finally, we gratefully acknowledge the cooperation and assistance of the Bureau of Labor Statistics in Washington, D.C. The authors alone are responsible for remaining errors and omissions.

PREFACE

In 1987, Hudson Institute published *Workforce 2000*, a study of the changing American workforce. Although "think tanks" seldom produce bestsellers, *Workforce 2000* proved the exception to the rule. Its sales approached 80,000 copies.

What explains *Workforce 2000*'s success in penetrating thousands of homes and generating hundreds of articles in response? It challenged the conventional wisdom. It showed that the workforce of the future would no longer consist primarily of white males in manufacturing jobs. Instead, women and minority workers would become increasingly more prominent. The book also pointed to the looming "skills gap" between what a well-educated labor force needed in a global economy and what a failing primary- and secondary-education system in the United States would equip workers to do.

Workforce 2000 thus placed the terms "skills gap" and "workplace diversity" on the national agenda. It issued four simple predictions, none of them obvious in 1987. All proved largely correct.

1. The U.S. economy would grow at a healthy pace, fueled by a rebound in U.S. exports, productivity growth, and a strong world economy.

In 1987 the Standard & Poor's 500-stock index stood at 338. It is up to 749 today. Annual U.S. exports more than doubled, going from $254 billion in 1987 to $584 billion in 1995. World Gross Domestic Product (GDP) per capita in constant dollars rose by more than 15 percent between 1987—when *Workforce 2000* was published—and 1994. U.S. GDP rose from $5.648 trillion in 1987 to $7 trillion in 1995 (in inflation-adjusted dollars).

In short, *Workforce 2000* was correct in its optimism.

2. Because of productivity gains, manufacturing would shrink as a share of employment in the U.S. But it would not "wither away."

Manufacturing has indeed declined as a share of U.S. employment. U.S. GDP is up by 54 percent since 1987. Even though manufacturing value added has risen 36 percent since 1987, the number of manufacturing employees is almost unchanged, because of productivity gains. But the bulk of job creation and economic growth has been in services.

Workforce 2000 was right again.

3. The workforce would grow slowly, becoming older and more female and including more minorities.

The employed civilian labor force increased by a modest 13 million between 1987 and 1995, and females accounted for two million more of the new workers than did men. Most new entrants into the workforce were still white males, but they largely replaced white males who were leaving it. As predicted, women and minorities made most of the net gains in employment.

4. *New jobs in service industries would demand much higher skill levels. Workforce 2000* said that very few new jobs would be available for those who could not read, follow directions, and use mathematics—another prediction that was clearly on the money.

Workforce 2000 was so straightforward that many informed readers read the book and concluded, "Well, of course, I knew that." Or, "Well, of course, I should have known that." Or perhaps, "If I had just paid a bit more attention, I could have known that." *Workforce 2000* was successful precisely because it was an "of course" book. It offered information that was familiar, but put it into a broader perspective.

But *Workforce 2000* also missed a few trends, as any crystal ball will. It omitted or downplayed several developments that now seem obvious.

1. The Digital Revolution

In 1987, IBM's first personal computer (PC) was barely five years old. The PC was still only a new and improved typewriter for everyone but a few hackers. Digital technologies had not yet begun to remake the workplace.

But PC prices soon tumbled as computing capability soared. In short order, PCs made their way into medium- and smaller-sized businesses and onto the desks of nonclerical employees. Cheap, worldwide long-distance communication made networked PCs a cost-effective tool for all sorts of business and personal applications.

Although *Workforce 2000* didn't completely miss the digital revolution, it did not fully anticipate its breadth and speed.

2. Geographic Disparities

Workforce 2000 looked more at overall trends than at specific geographical regions. So its findings said a lot about the overall, "macro" level but less about variations on the "micro" level. For example, ethnic populations are not spread evenly all across the country. Instead, minorities and immigrants tend to cluster in certain locales; there are many more Hispanics in California and the Southwest than elsewhere, and that will be even more true in the future. In a sense, Workforce 2000 told us more about the forest than about some very important individual trees.

3. The Diversity Industry

Ironically, *Workforce 2000* also missed a trend that stemmed from one of its very own—accurate—predictions. *Workforce 2000* foresaw the diversification of the workforce, as both women and minorities entered in greater proportions. But the authors did *not* predict that certain labor-force analysts would respond to this finding by spawning the diversity industry.

Workforce 2000 was "credited" with creating a diversity craze. To prepare for the increasingly diverse workforce that it foresaw, entrepreneurs responded by offering sensitivity training to accommodate cultural differences in the workplace. Government and industry began to hire well-paid diversity and sensitivity consultants in large numbers.

Many of these consultants argued that the new "nontraditional" workers would not be "underqualified," merely "differently qualified." In response, they contended, organizations would have to overcome a "white male" management ethic of conformity and assimilation.

But these diversity entrepreneurs misread *Workforce 2000* on two counts. First, they conveyed the impression that *Workforce 2000* predicted a scarcity of white (or white male) entrants to the workforce. In fact, white males are *still* prominent among *total* newcomers to the workforce. It's just that they are replacing the large numbers of white males who are leaving it as they age. On the other hand, the *net new entrants* to the workforce are from growing cohorts of women and minority workers—because the number of women and minorities leaving the workforce is currently far smaller. (To see our point, consider a hypothetical high school whose graduating senior class has 80 white males and 20 females and minorities. Now suppose that the entering freshman class has 80 white males and 30 women and minorities. The *total entrants* are dominated by the traditional group—those 80 white males. But the *net new entrants* to the student body consist of women and minorities—of whom there are now ten more.) Because *Workforce 2000*'s message was misunderstood, the impact of diversity was exaggerated: too much attention was paid to the women and minority net new entrants, too little to the white males among the total entrants.

The second major misreading of *Workforce 2000* concerned the needs of the nontraditional workers entering the workforce. *Workforce 2000* emphasized that the new entrants needed marketable skills, which the education system was not always providing. The result was the "skills gap." What new workers principally need—whether they are white and male or female and minority—are the skills that education must provide, not managers trained in diversity and sensitivity.

Why Workforce 2020?

Since *Workforce 2000* was so successful and so accurate, why do we offer a sequel? First, to incorporate newly available data. Although the original report continues to be used by human-resource personnel, corporate and government planners, and social-policy researchers, its data stem from the early 1980's. We now have fascinating new data measuring population growth and shifts in employment, and there is much to be said about changes in specific industries and occupations. Consider that some of the fastest growing occupations today—such as software and web-site development—didn't even exist in 1987.

We also write to counter serious misunderstandings about the future of our economy. Too many books and newspapers continue to purvey myths and half-truths like the following: jobs in manufacturing have disappeared; technology has dumbed down and destroyed jobs; wages are decreasing, so that the middle class is shrinking; a majority of tomorrow's workforce will consist of nonwhites and women; global trade has harmed American workers.

As you will see in what follows, none of these familiar assertions contains more than a grain of truth. Yet the widespread belief in them has generated solutions that are wrong-headed and counterproductive. Some policy analysts claim that workers need to be protected from globalization and from technological change; others call for stepped-up governmental efforts to counter race and gender discrimination that is thought to be endemic; still others advocate strengthening unions and expanding government bureaucracies. We believe that all of these policies are seriously misguided. By highlighting new data and perspectives, and by countering popular myths about our supposed economic plight, we hope to make the case against these ill-advised policies. Instead we argue for solutions that can create what we all desire—the most competitive workforce and economy in the world.

Executive Summary

An Introduction to
Workforce 2020

You have before you a map, one that describes the journey America's labor force is now beginning. It lays out the general contours of the employment landscape, not the fine details or the specific landmarks, depicting the many roads to what we call "Workforce 2020." Some will be superhighways and some will be dead ends for American workers. Although immense forces shape the employment landscape, we believe that we know the difference between the superhighways and the dead ends.

Skilled cartographers in the guise of economists, education experts, and policy researchers at Hudson Institute helped prepare this map. It offers our best ideas about what lies ahead and what Americans—collectively and individually, in large and small firms, in federal agencies and in small-town development commissions—should do to prepare for the journey to Workforce 2020.

Our map is needed because American workers at the threshold of the twenty-first century are embarking on mysterious voyages. They seek glittering destinations but travel along roads with numerous pitfalls and unexpected diversions. Many workers—more than at any time in America's history—will reach the glittering destinations. They will enjoy incomes unimaginable to their parents, along with working and living conditions more comfortable than anyone could have dreamed of in centuries past. But many other workers will be stymied by the pitfalls along the road or baffled by the diversions. Their standard of living may stagnate or even decline. Much is already known today about what will divide the hopeful from the anxious along these roads, and we will share that knowledge here.

What makes America's voyage to the workforce of 2020 unique is not merely the heights to which some will climb or the difficulties others will endure. Two qualities give a truly unprecedented character to the roads ahead. First, the gates have lifted before almost every American who wishes to embark on the journey of work. Age, gender, and race barriers to employment opportunity have broken down. What little conscious discrimination remains will be swept away soon—not by government regulation but by the enlightened self-interest of employers. Second, more and more individuals now undertake their own journeys through the labor force, rather than "hitching rides" on the traditional mass transportation provided by unions, large corporations, and government bureaucracies. For most workers, this "free agency" will be immensely liberating. But for others, it will provoke anxiety and anger. For all workers, the premium on education, flexibility, and foresight has never been greater than it will be in the years ahead.

What explains the immense satisfactions and dangers ahead? What makes possible the unprecedented expansion of opportunities in the labor force? What forces conspire, for better or worse, to demand that we compete as individuals and contend with ever-changing knowledge and skill requirements? We highlight four forces in particular.

FIRST, THE PACE OF TECHNOLOGICAL CHANGE in today's economy has never been greater. It will accelerate still further, in an exponential manner. Innovations in biotechnology, computing, telecommunications, and their confluences will bring new products and services that are at once marvelous and potentially frightening. And the "creative destruction" wrought by this technology on national economies, firms, and individual workers will be even more powerful in the twenty-first century than when economist Joseph Schumpeter coined the phrase fifty years ago. We cannot know what innovations will transform the global economy by 2020, any more than analysts in the mid-1970s could have foreseen the rise of the personal computer or the proliferation of satellite, fiber-optic, and wireless communications. However, the computer and telecommunications revolutions enable us to speculate in an informed manner on the implications of today's Innovation Age for the American workforce:

- Automation will continue to displace low-skilled or unskilled workers in America's manufacturing firms and offices. Indeed, machines will substitute for increasingly more sophisticated forms of human labor. Even firms that develop advanced technology will be able to replace some of their employees with technology (witness the "CASE tools" that now assist in writing routine computer code) or with lower-paid workers in other countries (witness the rise of India's computer programmers and data processors).

- However, experience suggests that the development, marketing, and servicing of ever more sophisticated products—and the use of those products in an ever richer ensemble of personal and professional services—almost certainly will create more jobs than the underlying technology will destroy. On the whole, the new jobs will also be safer, more stimulating, and better paid than the ones they replace.
- The best jobs created in the Innovation Age will be filled by Americans (and workers in other advanced countries) to the extent that workers possess the skills required to compete for them and carry them out. If jobs go unfilled in the U.S., they will quickly migrate elsewhere in our truly global economy.
- Because the best new jobs will demand brains rather than brawn, and because physical presence in a particular location at a particular time will become increasingly irrelevant, structural barriers to the employment of women and older Americans will continue to fall away. Americans of all backgrounds will be increasingly able to determine their own working environments and hours.

SECOND, THE REST OF THE WORLD MATTERS to a degree that it never did in the past. We can no longer say anything sensible about the prospects for American workers if we consider only the U.S. economy or the characteristics of the U.S. labor force. Fast-growing Asian and Latin American economies present us with both opportunities and challenges. Meanwhile, communications and transportation costs have plummeted (declining to almost zero in the case of information exchanged on the Internet), resulting in what some have called "the death of distance." Whereas the costs of shipping an automobile or a heavy machine tool remain consequential, the products of the world's most dynamic industries—such as biological formulas, computers, financial services, microchips, and software—can cross the globe for a pittance. Investment capital is also more abundant and more mobile than ever before, traversing borders with abandon in search of the best ideas, the savviest entrepreneurs, and the most productive economies. The implications of this globalization for U.S. workers are no less complex than the implications of new technology:

- Manufacturing will continue to dominate U.S. exports. Almost 20 percent of U.S. manufacturing workers now have jobs that depend on exports; that figure will continue to escalate. America's growing export dependence in the early twenty-first century will benefit most of America's highly productive workers, because many foreign economies will continue to expand more rapidly than our own, thereby generating massive demand for U.S. goods. Skilled workers whose jobs depend on exports are better paid than other U.S. manufacturing workers as a rule, because the U.S. enjoys a comparative advantage in the specialized manufacturing and service sectors that create their jobs. These workers also tend to earn more than similar workers in other countries.

- But globalization will affect low-skilled or unskilled American workers very differently. They will compete for jobs and wages not just with their counterparts across town or in other parts of the U.S., but also with low-skilled workers around the globe. As labor costs become more important to manufacturers than shipping costs, the U.S. will retain almost no comparative advantage in low-skilled manufacturing. Jobs in that sector will disappear or be available only at depressed wages. Second or third jobs and full-time employment for both spouses—already the norm in households headed by low-skilled workers—will become even more necessary.

- Manufacturing's share of total U.S. employment will continue to decline, due to the combined effects of automation and globalization. But the millions of high-productivity manufacturing jobs that remain will be more highly skilled and therefore better paid than at any other time in U.S. history. Employment growth, meanwhile, will remain concentrated in services, which also will benefit increasingly from export markets and will offer high salaries for skilled workers.

- Globalization and technological change will make most segments of the U.S. economy extremely volatile, as comparative advantages in particular market segments rise and then fall away. Small- and medium-sized firms will be well situated to react to this volatility, and their numbers will grow. Labor unions will cope badly with this rapidly evolving economy of small producers, and their membership and influence will shrink. Individual workers will change jobs frequently over time. For those who maintain and improve their skills, the changes should bring increasing rewards. But the changes may be traumatic for those who fall behind the skills curve and resist retraining.

THIRD, AMERICA IS GETTING OLDER. At some level, all of us are aware of this. Our parents and grandparents are living longer, and we are having fewer children. But U.S. public policy as well as many employers have yet to come to grips with the full implications of America's aging. The oldest among America's so-called baby boomers—the massive cohort born between 1945 and 1965—will begin to reach age 65 in 2010. By 2020, almost 20 percent of the U.S. population will be 65 or older. There will be as many Americans of "retirement age" as there are 20-35-year-olds. America's aging baby boomers will decisively affect the U.S. workforce, through their departure from and continued presence in it, and as recipients of public entitlements and purchasers of services:

- America's taxpayer-funded entitlements for its aging population—Medicare and Social Security—are likely to undergo profound changes in the next two decades. The tax rates necessary to sustain the current "pay-as-you-go" approach to funding these programs as the baby boomers retire will rise, perhaps precipitously, unless the expectations of retirees regarding their benefits become more modest, the economy grows more strongly than expected, or the programs receive fundamental overhauls.
- Depending on how the funding of entitlement programs is resolved and how well individual baby boomers have prepared for retirement, some who reach age 65 will continue to require

outside income and will be unable to retire. Many others will not want to retire and will seek flexible work options. As average life expectancies extend past 80 years of age, even many of the well-heeled will conclude that twenty years on golf courses and cruise ships do not present enough of a challenge.

- Whether they continue working or simply enjoy the fruits of past labors, America's aging baby boomers will constitute a large and powerful segment of the consumer market. Their resulting demand for entertainment, travel, and other leisure-time pursuits; specialized health care; long-term care facilities; and accounting, home-repair, and other professional services will fuel strong local labor markets throughout the U.S., but particularly in cities and regions that attract many retirees. The jobs created by this boom in the service sector in local economies may replace many of the low-skilled or unskilled manufacturing jobs the U.S. stands to lose, though not always at comparable wages.

FOURTH, THE U.S. LABOR FORCE continues its ethnic diversification, though at a fairly slow pace. Most white non-Hispanics entering America's early twenty-first century workforce simply will replace exiting white workers; minorities will constitute slightly more than half of net new entrants to the U.S. workforce. Minorities will account for only about a third of total new entrants over the next decade. Whites constitute 76 percent of the total labor force today and will account for 68 percent in 2020. The share of African-Americans in the labor force probably will remain constant, at 11 percent, over the next twenty years. The Asian and Hispanic shares will grow to 6 and 14 percent, respectively. Most of this change will be due to the growth of Asian and Hispanic workforce representation in the South and West. The changes will not be dramatic on a national scale. The aging of the U.S. workforce will be far more dramatic than its ethnic shifts.

In summary, Hudson Institute's *Workforce 2020* offers a vision of a bifurcated U.S. labor force in the early twenty-first century. As we envision the next twenty-plus years, the skills premium appears even more powerful to us than it did to our predecessors who wrote *Workforce 2000.* Millions of Americans with proficiency in math, science, and the

English language will join a global elite whose services will be in intense demand. These workers will command generous and growing compensation. Burgeoning local markets for services in some parts of the U.S. will continue to sustain some decent-paying, low-skill jobs. But other Americans with inadequate education and no technological expertise—how many depends in large part on what we do to improve their training—will face declining real wages or unemployment, particularly in manufacturing.

Much can be done to improve the prospects of America's twenty-first century workforce. The challenges are not simple, however, and the Workforce 2020 team therefore rejects the simple responses that have become so prevalent of late. These simple responses involve using public policy to build walls around industries, technology, and people. Such walls of protectionism cannot make the world go away or stave off the effects of human inventiveness. Indeed, the effort to build such walls will almost always have the perverse effect of making the intended beneficiaries worse off.

The protection of older, low-wage industries generally benefits owners more than workers in those industries, by handing them what amounts to unearned profits. It raises consumer prices throughout the economy and slows the dissemination of new knowledge through the market while merely postponing the inevitable reckoning with world markets. Efforts to slow the application of labor-saving technology limit the competitiveness of key industries and perpetuate jobs that are more dangerous and tedious than the ones that would replace them. Finally, public-policy efforts to regulate hiring and firing accomplish nothing more than to give temporary comfort to those who already have jobs. Western Europe—with its persistent double-digit unemployment in most countries—is a massive case study on the negative effects of extreme labor-force regulation on the creation of new jobs.

To reject simple, protectionist responses is not to accept the status quo. There is much that American policymakers, business leaders, and workers themselves can do to steer the country's labor force in the direction of even greater prosperity and security. After making sure that the challenges are understood—and we consider this book a contribution to that goal—the possible remedies can be grouped into three categories:

expanding the pool of workers; increasing workforce participation; and, most importantly, promoting upward mobility. All three sets of remedies begin with the premise that an aging America needs to increase its supply of highly skilled workers willing to enter or remain in the labor force.

One way to ensure that America's jobs get done is to increase the pool of skilled workers. To that end, U.S. firms should press for enlightened immigration policies that give preference to skilled workers. It is simply false that immigrants steal jobs from Americans at the higher ends of the job ladder. To the contrary, America's most dynamic, high-tech industries have come to depend on immigrants as well as U.S. citizens, and they will continue to do so in the future. Instead of providing key industries with large numbers of highly educated immigrants, however, U.S. immigration policy serves primarily to increase the number of U.S. residents who lack even a high-school degree. America must stop recruiting workers for jobs that do not exist or exist only at the lowest wages.

Increasing workforce participation is the other route to filling demand for highly skilled workers. This has two dimensions. Firms and governments will be well advised to accommodate unconventional working arrangements that encourage parents with strong job skills to remain in (or re-enter) the workforce. Flexible hours and the option of working at home, for example, are accommodations permitted by today's technology and the nature of many kinds of twenty-first century jobs. Similarly, the most successful firms of the early twenty-first century will find ways to benefit from the experience and talents of older workers. Retaining workers who are eligible, but perhaps not truly ready to retire will be a human-resource challenge involving a wide array of compensation and benefits issues as well as demanding changes in Medicare, Social Security, and tax laws.

Expanding the pool and participation of skilled labor is vital, but positive scenarios for Workforce 2020 depend most of all on the promotion of mobility. An America with a large number of workers who are unemployable or capable of working only in the most menial, low-wage jobs will be an America fraught with social tension and burdened by expensive demands on social-welfare programs. Upward mobility in the labor force depends, quite simply, on education. The single most important goal of workforce development must be to improve the quality of American public education substantially.

This report concludes with several recommendations concerning higher education. The Workforce 2020 team documents the compensation and mobility benefits of higher education, but we part company with those who would create an entitlement to two (or more) years of college. College cannot remedy the deficiencies of primary and secondary education. Nor is it an appropriate path for many prospective workers who would be better served by solid vocational training. The crucial factor accounting for long-term success in the workforce is a basic education provided at the primary and secondary levels—encompassing the ability to read and write, do basic math, solve problems, and behave dependably. Too often, this education is not made available to America's young people, and too often, parents and employers fail to acknowledge the shortcomings of public education in their own communities until it is too late.

Public schools need to set high academic standards for all children, regardless of their family backgrounds. Rewards for administrators, teachers, and students must accompany the attainment of those standards, and negative consequences must accompany failure. In addition, America must consider alternatives to the prevailing nineteenth century approach to the delivery of public education, which resembles an old factory assembly line in many ways and does little to recognize the different abilities and needs of students. Injecting competition into public education is, in our view, the best way to encourage alternative approaches without imposing a single new model from on high. Charter schools and voucher programs are two very promising means of promoting such competition, and we endorse them strongly.

The journey to Workforce 2020 is a journey to an uncertain destination. In twenty years, observers may conclude that the American dream has never worked better, increasing the prosperity of millions of people and utilizing the talents of the nation in a manner that promotes general well-being. But the road map laid out here could lead to another, more disturbing destination, in which America divides more than ever into a society of haves and have-nots based on access to the best jobs, and in which a large share of the population is idled by unemployment or premature retirement. Fortunately, though our destination remains uncertain from the vantage point of the late 1990s, we believe that there is much that policymakers, corporate officials, and every other American can do to steer the nation in the right direction.

CHAPTER ONE
THE FORCES SHAPING THE AMERICAN ECONOMY

The American economy is a $7-trillion leviathan in the late 1990s. By 2020, even if it grows by only 2.5 percent per year, its Gross Domestic Product (GDP) will have reached $11.5 trillion in 1997 dollars. Other than being much larger, how will the American economy differ from what it is today? It will be reshaped by the following five forces:

- Rapid technological change;
- Further global integration of the U.S. economy;
- Rapid economic growth in certain developing nations;
- Deregulation and liberalization, both nationally and globally; and
- Demographic change, especially the aging of the baby boomers.

Operating together, these forces will continue to alter the face of the American economy in the following ways:

- Markets for products, services, and capital will become broader and deeper.
- Monopoly will decrease and competition will increase throughout the economy.
- Local markets for goods and services will expand.
- The shift from goods production to service production will continue.

To understand the meaning and significance of these changes, we must first examine the forces that are producing them.

Rapid Technological Change—The Seminal Force

Rapid technological change is upon us, as it has been since the beginning of the Industrial Revolution 250 years ago. As was true in the past, new industries and occupations are being created, while old ones are rendered obsolete—the "creative destruction" discussed by Joseph Schumpeter.[1] Labor and capital flow from declining to emerging industries; productivity increases; and average living standards rise. What is new today is that the pace of technological change is accelerating.

What will be the impact of technological change on the American economy, on its jobs and workers, in the early twenty-first century? The twenty-first century picture, like earlier ones, will be mixed. Technological change will bring both winners and losers among industries, companies, occupations, and individuals. Although many outcomes are bound to come as surprises, it is safe to say that technological change will affect workplaces and the workforce in multiple and often contradictory ways.

How does technology change things? To begin with, it alters *productive processes*, i.e., the way work is done: it typically increases productivity and reduces the costs of production. Simply put, more output is produced with less input.

But new technology does not mean that less use is made of every type of input. In fact, a new technology may increase the use of some inputs. For example, vastly less labor but much more energy is used to produce America's food today than fifty years ago. Mechanized agriculture has had a *direct* labor-saving effect; there are fewer farmers today, as machines have been substituted for labor. But those machines have also caused increased use of a second input—fossil fuels. It is also important to realize that mechanization has had significant *indirect* impacts on employment that have added new jobs; human labor is needed to produce the machines and energy that today's agriculture demands.

Technology also changes the products themselves, i.e., the goods and services that the economy generates. For example, personal computers (PCs) did not exist until the 1980s; today, millions of workers manufacture, distribute, and service them. This is no isolated example;

entirely new industries, companies, and occupations routinely arise to provide things that previously did not exist. Virtually no one in 1980, for example, had heard of Microsoft; the packaged software industry had not yet come into being. But that industry is growing rapidly today, and Microsoft is one of the world's largest corporations.

Here, too, the direct and indirect effects can differ dramatically. New products always mean new jobs and expanded employment in the industries that produce them. But their introduction may indirectly cost jobs, as less labor-intensive new products are substituted for more labor-intensive old ones, causing employment to drop in established industries.

Furthermore, technological change does not always save on every kind of labor or the same kind of labor. Recent technological change in America has tended to require more workers who are highly skilled, but fewer low-skilled ones. But in the past, the technological changes that underlay the early growth of assembly-line manufacturing increased the demand for unskilled labor.

The Impact of Information Technology on the Economy

Having noted that the changes induced by technology can run in many different directions, can we say anything more about their likely future course? One thing at least seems certain—the continued and increased predominance of the information technology (IT) industries, those spawned by the confluence of computer science and telecommunications. IT, which has already drastically reshaped the American economy, will only increase its impact in years to come: at the end of this chapter we illustrate some of its likely effects by examining specific industries in the service sector.

IT's impact has been spurred by remarkable success in miniaturizing computers, resulting from the placement of many transistors and other electronic components on a tiny silicon wafer or "chip." In 1965, Gordon E. Moore, cofounder of the semiconductor company Intel, propounded "Moore's Law," according to which chip density—the number of transistors that can be packed on a single microchip—doubles about every eighteen months (see Figure 1-1). From a mere 65,000 in the late 1970s, chip density will reach 125 million transistors before the end of

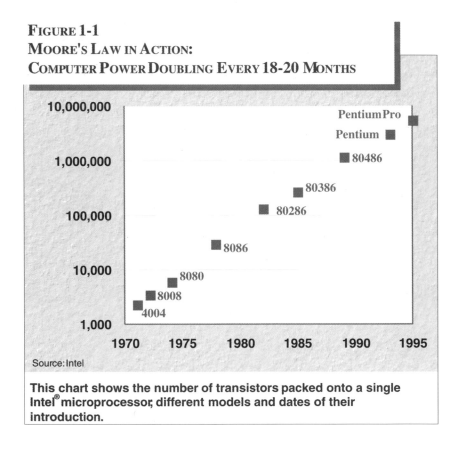

FIGURE 1-1
MOORE'S LAW IN ACTION:
COMPUTER POWER DOUBLING EVERY 18-20 MONTHS

Source: Intel

This chart shows the number of transistors packed onto a single Intel® microprocessor, different models and dates of their introduction.

this century. New technologies in the early twenty-first century may even make Moore's Law look overly cautious.

Soaring chip densities are mirrored by plummeting costs of data storage and computation. A 1975-model IBM mainframe computer could carry out 10 million instructions per second and cost about $10 million. By 1995 an ordinary desktop computer employing a Pentium microprocessor could compute nearly seven times that fast and cost only about $3,000. In cost/performance terms, the capital cost of performing one million instructions had dropped from $1 million in 1975 to $45 in 1995, a decline of more than 99.99 percent in the span of twenty years. If the price of automobiles had dropped at a corresponding rate, 1975's $100,000 Rolls Royce would have cost $4.50 in 1995!

An input whose cost declines relative to others' is used more intensively; it is substituted for more expensive inputs whenever possible. The rapidly plunging costs of IT have dramatically increased its attractiveness to businesses of the most diverse kinds and thus sparked an explosive growth of its use in both productive processes and new products. Computers and telecommunications are increasingly used in the production and distribution of virtually every American good and service. In addition, new IT products ranging from compact discs to global positioning systems are finding their way into consumer and producer usage.

IT Offers Clues for the Future

With IT now so pervasive, it is reasonable to suppose that the IT industries themselves can serve as something like a "leading indicator" for the rest of the economy: developments destined for the overall American economy occur earlier, faster, and in more exaggerated form in the IT industries. By looking at the recent past and likely future of these IT industries, we can draw important conclusions about the probable impact of IT's continuing conquest of the American economy. Will IT create or destroy jobs? Will it elevate or lower the quality of jobs and the wages they pay? Judging from the evidence offered by the IT industries, the answers to these questions are many and sometimes contradictory.

Consider first the *semiconductor industry*, which designs and produces integrated circuits.[2] This industry boomed in the 1970s and early 1980s. Technological advances in integrated circuitry and computer design came rapidly. New firms sprouted, production soared, and employment grew by approximately 240 percent, reaching nearly 300,000 by 1985. But labor-saving IT technology was advancing rapidly in the semiconductor industry itself. Output continued to expand rapidly after 1985 but employment fell, because chip makers were automating the production of labor-intensive integrated circuits. International specialization developed: U.S. producers such as Intel and Motorola developed a strong comparative advantage in the design and manufacture of central processing units (CPUs, the chips that do a computer's "thinking"), but the production of memory chips shifted abroad, where labor costs were lower.

As for the future, U.S. semiconductor production is projected to grow rapidly, at about 8 percent annually, at least until 2005. But unlike the late 1980s, employment will also increase. Indeed, employment has been heading upward since 1993. In addition, the semiconductor jobs of today and tomorrow are very different from those of the 1970s and 1980s. The exacting but highly repetitive jobs of yesterday, such as soldering circuit boards, are now done mainly by machines or inexpensive workers overseas. Most jobs in tomorrow's semiconductor industry will require high skills, in fields such as research and development, chip design, capital-intensive microprocessor production, and maintenance. The American companies that now dominate the design and manufacture of the machines used to produce integrated circuits employ more workers who are highly qualified.

The workforce outlook for the American semiconductor industry into the early twenty-first century poses both a promise and a problem. The promise is that the high-skilled jobs that are expanding will pay well, much better than the relatively unskilled jobs that were lost to machines and foreign workers in the 1980s and early 1990s.

The problem is that these skilled workers are in short supply. American semiconductor companies are already finding it difficult to fill the positions available, particularly at entry levels. If America is to retain these high-skilled, well-paying jobs (and not see them gravitate to places like Singapore, which are avidly bidding for them by upgrading the skills of local workers), more American workers will have to command the requisite workplace skills.

In short, jobs have been both created and destroyed in the semiconductor industry at a dizzying pace. But the jobs that were lost required comparatively few skills, whereas the jobs that have been (and will be) created are both better-paying and higher-skilled. In these respects the semiconductor industry highlights trends that characterize the entire American economy.

Turn now to the computer industry, which also offers an extraordinary if exaggerated illustration of the forces shaping the American economy.[3] Since 1945 this industry has been swept by repeated waves of technology-driven "creative destruction." The industry has been marked by increasingly fierce competition among both domestic and foreign producers, soaring growth of output, plunging product prices, ever shorter product life cycles (as products are rendered obsolete not long after being designed), and general frenetic change.

In 1994 the computer industry accounted for a modest 2.1 percent of value added in U.S. manufacturing and only 1.9 percent of all manufacturing employment. Those percentages are substantially down from the 1982 figures, 2.8 percent and 2.1 percent, respectively. And they pale in comparison to the automobile industry's 13.5 percent and 4.2 percent.[4] This raises a question: If the IT industries are growing so rapidly, why does the computer industry account for such a small and declining share of manufacturing employment and output?

Actually, employment in the computer industry skyrocketed until 1984. Large job growth followed major technological innovations, as American producers dominated world production of all kinds of computers, from mainframes to personal computers (PCs). Between the appearance of the first PC in the mid-1970s and 1982, computer-industry jobs grew by nearly 80 percent while total U.S. manufacturing employment was growing by only 4 percent.[5] But in the mid-1980s jobs began to disappear: through the next decade, employment in the American computer industry declined by an average annual rate of about 3 percent.

Technology explains the dramatic post-1982 job losses. First, the structure of the industry changed drastically. Mainframes and minicomputers dominated usage at the beginning of the 1980s; personal computers began their steep ascent only after IBM introduced its PC in 1981. But a horde of other companies soon began to produce "IBM compatible" machines. The avalanche of these so-called clones quickly drove down PC prices, forcing all PC makers to rush more powerful models to market, lest they be overwhelmed by the competition.

As PC prices plunged while performance rose rapidly, computer users began a massive switch to PCs, causing mainframe and minicomputer manufacturers to reel. Their profits evaporating, some traditional computer manufacturers left the industry (e.g., Honeywell and Wang), while others sought viability by downsizing: Digital Equipment Corporation (DEC) cut tens of thousands of jobs, and IBM also laid off workers.

Meanwhile, intense competition among PC makers sent profit margins sharply downward. As in the semiconductor industry, this competitive pressure sent American computer-makers scurrying to cut production costs. Automation was used more extensively, and product assembly, which remained more labor-intensive, was transferred to plants in Taiwan and other Asian countries. The final, globalized result: American makers of CPUs export many of their products, even as most assembled PCs are themselves imported.

For the computer industry's workforce, the results have been wrenching. Total employment fell by 26 percent between 1983 and 1994, and it will fall by another 25 percent by 2005.[6] Production workers, who comprised more than 43 percent of all employees in the industry in 1975, made up only about 35 percent twenty years later.[7] Most jobs in the computer industry are now and increasingly will be in the areas of research and development, design, engineering, software, and customer support. All these jobs require higher-order skills than the production jobs that are being lost.

Furthermore, the disappearance of production jobs is not a cause for gloom, because it has been coupled by the emergence of other positions. The computer industry's sharp decline in production jobs since the mid-1980s has been more than compensated for by job gains in the retail stores that sell computers (up 73 percent between 1987 and 1993). Likewise, in firms that supply computer and data-processing services increased by 68 percent over the same period.[8]

Thus the large and highly publicized downsizings among *Fortune* 500 computer companies have been more than made up for by new hirings in relatively small retail and service firms. Selling software, training, maintenance, and other support services is often more profitable than selling computers themselves.

What does the future hold for the industry? It will continue to grow. Even though almost all businesses will be computerized by the beginning of the twenty-first century, the business market will still not be saturated. As prices keep falling while performance improves, businesses will find new and expanded uses for computers.

But it is the home market for computers, software, and services that will grow most rapidly during the next decade. Approximately 40 percent of American households owned computers in early 1996; by the year 2000 the figure is likely to exceed 60 percent.[9] By 2010, when American consumers' computer, television, wireless, and other telecommunications network services will be increasingly integrated and supplied by a large number of avidly competing providers, 90 percent of households will own computers. Even that impressively high total will leave room for growth; after all, 98 percent of households now own televisions.

The workforce implications of this wholesale computer invasion of American businesses and homes will be profound. As previously discussed, jobs in computer hardware and software sales and service will expand impressively. Other areas of high job growth, at least in the near term, will be in software and content development. U.S. firms enjoy extremely favorable competitive positions in the global markets for these products.

Job growth in American software companies is now explosive and will remain buoyant at least for the next several years. Employment in the prepackaged software industry doubled between 1988 and 1994, and increased by another 15 percent in 1995. Home education and entertainment software will enjoy the most rapid sales increases in the late 1990s; well before the year 2000 the sales of such applications will have topped sales of software such as word processing aimed at the office market.[10] Another IT technology, that of the CD ROM, is now on an exponential growth curve and will heavily drive the demand for software. The skilled labor required to produce these products can make effective use of ever cheaper and more powerful IT.

Dramatically improving price/performance ratios have spurred IT innovation across a broad front for more than two decades and have thus stimulated the demand for the skilled labor (e.g., that of software engineers, programmers, and systems analysts) that employs the technology. Jobs in computer services increased nearly tenfold between 1972 and the mid-1990s, exceeding one million in 1995.[11] These new skilled and well-paying jobs more than counterbalance the less skilled computer-industry jobs lost because of advances in the same technology.

Even some of these highly skilled positions, however, may ultimately be lost. The growing power of computers makes possible more sophisticated software tools that assist in or even automate significant aspects of software development itself. These tools carry acronyms such as CASE (computer-aided software engineering), AI (artificial intelligence), and CAD (computer-assisted design). Such technological progress increases productivity by requiring less labor; but in this case the labor to be eliminated is performed by skilled software engineers and programmers. In short, as the technology continues to develop, it can replace human labor in carrying out increasingly more complicated tasks.

The easiest and, therefore, earliest software development tasks to be delegated to CASE are the most structured and routine programming jobs. On the other hand, it is hard to automate the creative, unstructured, problem-solving tasks that comprise the artistic heart of software engineering. That will be the last redoubt of human activity to yield to CASE—if it ever does.

American jobs in software engineering have also increased in response to the developing global market in computer services. Traditional services, unlike physical goods, could not be transported from one place to another. Most could be delivered only when the person delivering the services was near the place or person receiving them. Very few services were ever internationally tradeable. Like most other services, software development and other computer services could not be exported or imported. That is now changing.

The extraordinary development of IT is eroding geographical barriers to the exchange of computer services and engineering. Since the mid-1980s, international trade in these services has boomed, much to the advantage of the U.S. balance of trade. The combined trade surplus in these two areas more than tripled between 1986 and 1994 to $4.7 billion.[12]

U.S. computer and engineering services will continue to expand rapidly into the early twenty-first century. Although imports are likely to increase at a faster rate, they will start from a very small base. America's trade surplus in these services will therefore grow for a decade or more. As these net exports grow, so too will the number of jobs in the computer services and engineering industries that serve foreign markets.

The globalization of IT means that more programmers in India and other foreign nations will provide software and other engineering services to American customers. But the most creative and unstructured work will continue to be done on these shores. Cultural obstacles to international cooperation in software development will remain, long after telecommunications advances have destroyed the geographical barriers. Only the least complex software-development tasks are likely to be delegated to programmers and engineers abroad; more complex software will probably still be created here. Thus foreign competition in these fields will displace some journeyman programming and engineering jobs in the United States but will do little to inhibit the rapid growth in this area of highly skilled employment.

By no means, however, will foreign workers be absent from the American computer and engineering service industries; they will be present as immigrants working in the U.S. Skilled foreign engineers and computer specialists have been drawn to work here for many decades. The payrolls of leading IT companies such as Intel and Microsoft include many highly skilled, foreign-born employees. In their absence it would be difficult for America to retain its global lead in IT.

What have we learned from this survey of developments in the American computer industry? The following crucial factors are worthy of notice:

- Rapid technological progress and increasingly fierce competition have spurred productivity and caused jobs to be created and disappear very quickly. Companies and workers in the IT industries have had to learn to anticipate and respond to rapid changes in the business and work environments.

- The American computer industry has shifted from manufacturing computers to providing computer services. The jobs lost here as computers began to be manufactured overseas have been amply replaced by new jobs in servicing computers and computer users.

- The new jobs pay better and require higher skills than the jobs that have been lost in the industry.

- The job gains and losses are largely explained by the globalization of the computer industry. We are increasingly producing goods and services to be sold abroad, and importing goods and services from abroad. The goods we import are produced by relatively low-skilled labor. Our exports of computer goods and services are growing rapidly; the jobs generated by our exports pay better and require higher skills than the jobs lost to foreign competition.

- Globalization also means that the good jobs being created can "migrate" abroad if other countries upgrade the skills of their workforces more effectively than we do. To maintain our workforce superiority, we must continue to welcome highly skilled immigrant workers to our shores.

It is important to realize that the trends outlined here do not apply only to the computer industry. Because the computer industry is crucial for the whole American economy, developments such as these are occurring increasingly in many other industries as well.

Further Global Integration of the U.S. Economy

Pervasive technological change, especially in communications and transportation, affects the American economy as a whole. As distance poses fewer difficulties for transactions, previously separate markets merge. The resulting global integration—already evident in our survey of the IT industries—is a second major force shaping the American economy.

Global transportation and communications costs have plummeted in this century, and the decline has accelerated since the 1950s (see Figure 1-2). For example, the cost of a three-minute New York-to-London telephone conversation dropped six-fold between 1940 and 1970, and another tenfold from 1970 to 1990.

By the late 1990s the marginal costs of communicating globally via the Internet had plunged to zero for most users. The early twenty-first century will bring ever greater integration of voice, data, and television signals. Together with further deregulation of the world's telecommunication industries, this integration ensures that the user cost of global communications will continue to drop. Long before 2020, people in cities as far apart as New York and New Delhi will exchange almost unlimited quantities of information easily and inexpensively. By then, the demise of distance will be virtually complete.

Thus technology will broaden the boundaries of many markets for goods and services far beyond their former local or regional limits. These expanded markets will attract new buyers and sellers, who will participate on an equal footing. At its core, globalization is about broadening markets to include more participants.

FIGURE 1-2
TRANSPORT AND COMMUNICATIONS COSTS
HAVE PLUMMETED IN THE 20TH CENTURY

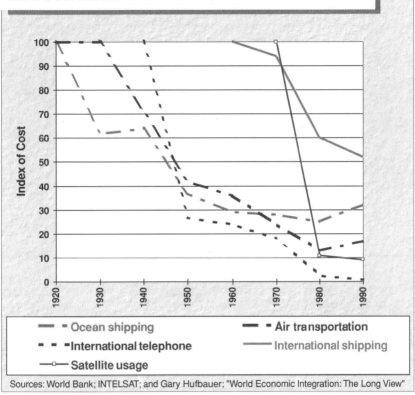

Sources: World Bank; INTELSAT; and Gary Hufbauer; "World Economic Integration: The Long View"

As markets have opened across the globe in recent years, the volume of goods and services traded across national borders has expanded. Indeed, international trade is rapidly outpacing world economic growth. Between 1980 and 1995, for example, total world output grew by approximately 60 percent. Meanwhile, international trade grew by about 120 percent, or twice as fast as output (see Figure 1-3). The ratio of world trade to world GDP grew three times more quickly in the period 1985-1994 than in the preceding ten years, and nearly three times as fast as in the 1960's. About 25 percent of annual world output was traded internationally in 1970; that figure will grow to 50 percent in 2000 and may approach 67 percent in 2020.

FIGURE 1-3
WORLD TRADE OUTPACES WORLD OUTPUT GROWTH
(ANNUAL PERCENTAGE CHANGE)

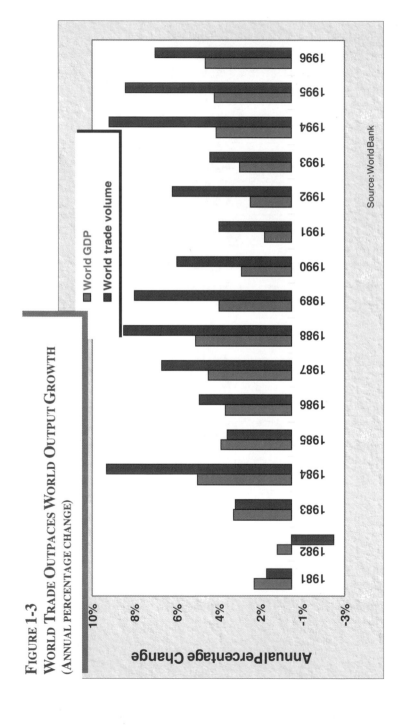

Source: World Bank

FIGURE 1-4
FOREIGN TRADE ALSO GROWS IN THE U.S.

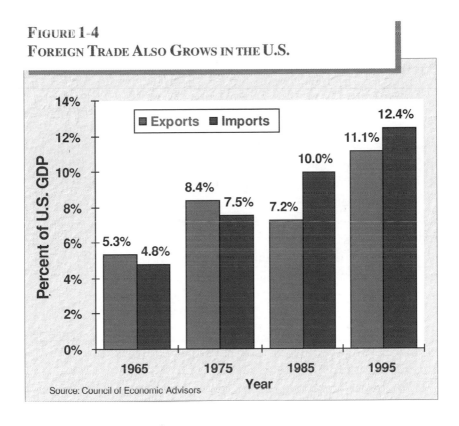

Source: Council of Economic Advisors

International trade is also becoming more important for the United States. As Figure 1-4 shows, exports grew from about 5 percent of GDP in 1965 to more than 11 percent by 1995. Imports, meanwhile, grew from 4.8 percent of GDP to 12.4 percent. By the mid-1990s, in other words, foreign trade played a role in the American economy that was between two and three times as important as it had been in 1965.

Manufacturing is, by far, our largest export sector. Contrary to the conventional perception that the United States has ceased to be a global manufacturing power, America's factories have expanded their share of total exports from 51 percent in 1970 to 57 percent in 1995.[13] We now export fewer primary products (farm and forestry products and other raw materials)—not fewer manufactured goods.

The Share of America's Manufacturing Workers with Export-Related Jobs is Large and Rising

In 1969 fewer than 4 percent of all U.S. manufacturing workers held export-related jobs; by 1981 that share had jumped to 12.8 percent. By 1991 the total had climbed further, to 18.6 percent.[14] If present trends continue, the figure will exceed 25 percent by 2000 and could approach 50 percent by 2010. This remarkable development runs directly counter to the conventional wisdom: American manufacturing is *not* in decline. Instead, increasingly it produces goods for sale on global markets.

Manufacturing increasingly dominates U.S. exports, and as Table 1-1 indicates, this trend is even more pronounced in certain industries. Between 1975 and 1991 (the last year for which data are available) the number of American workers employed in export-related work increased in every major manufacturing industry except tobacco products. And in some industries export-related jobs have grown phenomenally. In printing and publishing, for example, export-related employment grew by 925 percent in those sixteen years. In electric and electronic equipment manufacturing, export-related work accounted for more than one-third of all jobs in 1991.

Thus American manufacturing is integrating into global markets at a furious pace. The share of U.S. manufacturing jobs that depend on export markets is large and rising very rapidly. Economic globalization, so often vilified as the enemy of well-paying manufacturing jobs in this country, is in fact its strongest ally. The much-bemoaned exodus of U.S. manufacturing jobs offshore represents the export of low-productivity jobs that America should be happy to exchange for high-productivity and better-paying jobs. In short, the future of manufacturing in America depends on the continued rapid growth of exports.

Globalization Greatly Benefits America

In 1776, when the United States declared itself a separate nation, the economist Adam Smith published *The Wealth of Nations*. A central tenet of that famous tome was that individuals and nations enrich themselves

TABLE 1-1
U.S. MANUFACTURING JOBS
    DEPEND INCREASINGLY ON EXPORTS

Specific Industry	Number of export-related jobs in 1991 (thousands)	Percent gain from 1976 to 1991	Percent of all jobs in this industry in 1991
Electric, electronic equipment	484	147%	33.9%
Chemicals	221	195%	29.3%
Textiles	85	204%	28.8%
Transportation equipment	377	86%	26.2%
Apparel	61	281%	23.1%
Leather, leather products	15	150%	23.1%
Tobacco products	9	-10%	20.3%
Machinery, except electric	512	74%	19.0%
Misc. manufacturing	49	96%	18.8%
Printing & publishing	123	925%	16.6%
Primary metals	198	560%	14.3%
Paper & allied products	87	314%	14.0%
Lumber & wood products	105	357%	13.7%
Stone, clay, glass products	51	200%	13.6%
Fabricated metal products	256	266%	10.7%
Petroleum and coal products	11	267%	10.1%
Food and kindred products	91	146%	8.2%
Rubber & plastics	160	596%	6.3%
Instruments	193	141%	6.2%
Furniture & fixtures	24	380%	5.2%
Total, all manufacturing industries	3,363	187%	18.6%

Source: *Statistical Abstract of the United States, 1979 & 1996*

by specializing in what they do best: the division of labor promotes wealth creation by facilitating specialization. Nations gain from international trade, Smith pointed out, because trade allows each to concentrate its resources on what it does best.

A few decades later another British economist, David Ricardo, developed Smith's insight by distinguishing the concepts of *absolute advantage* and *comparative advantage*. Ricardo pointed out that trade is based on comparative advantage. Suppose, for example, that an attorney were more highly skilled at both word processing and litigating than any applicant for a secretarial job. The attorney then enjoys an *absolute* advantage over the job applicants in both kinds of work. But does that mean that the attorney should not hire a secretary? Obviously not. The attorney might be better at both kinds of work, but his or her superiority in litigating is greater than it is in word processing. It therefore makes sense to hire a secretary, so that the lawyer can specialize in what he or she has been specifically trained to do. The attorney is said to have a *comparative advantage* in litigating, while the secretary has one in word processing.

We all understand comparative advantage in our daily lives, as when we buy our groceries rather than produce our own food. It is not sufficiently understood, though, that trade among nations is advantageous for the same reason. Globalization is good for America because it allows us to specialize in producing those goods and services in which we have the greatest comparative advantage. By enabling us to use our labor and other resources in industries and occupations in which our productivity is highest and growing rapidly, globalization helps raise incomes and living standards in America.

At the same time, it is obviously true that globalization harms some individual Americans. In the textile industry, for example, employment dropped from one million in 1969 to 635,000 in 1996, despite strongly protectionist U.S. trade polices.[15] American workers who have lost their jobs because we now import more clothes from developing countries have indeed suffered.

But the remedy for their pain is not artificially and indefinitely to maintain employment in relatively low-productivity jobs in industries in which other nations have a comparative advantage. Instead, America's challenge is rapidly to move as many displaced workers as possible into

producing goods and services in which we enjoy the comparative advan
tage and where both productivity and pay are higher. Unfortunately,
workers who have lost jobs due to import competition often do not live
in the regions where jobs are gained when export-related industries
expand. Our labor markets will have to become more flexible if we are
to do better in matching workers and jobs.

Export-Related Jobs Pay Well

As a rule, export-related jobs pay much better than those lost to
import competition. Indeed, high-tech manufacturing jobs pay nearly
one-fourth better than jobs in other manufacturing industries.[16] No one
should be surprised by this statistic, which is consistent with economic
theory. Compared to the rest of the world, America enjoys a relative
abundance of highly skilled workers employed in specialized manufacturing and service sectors (such as IT or aircraft production), in which high
technology is the norm. U.S. exports are heavily concentrated in machinery, vehicles, scientific equipment, pharmaceuticals, and other high-tech
manufactured goods. The United States has a comparative advantage in
these sectors, but not in those employing mainly low-skilled and poorly
paid workers.

*America's Foreign Trade Deficit Reflects Our Low National
Savings Rate and the Nation's Attractiveness to Foreign Investors*

Our persistent foreign trade deficit is often blamed on other nations'
"discriminatory" trade practices or "unfair" competition from low-wage
countries. In fact, the trade deficit results directly from the fact that
America produces less than it consumes and invests.

The root cause of our trade deficits is the fact that we save less than
we invest. To pay for our desired levels of investment, we borrow from
foreigners. Total savings as a percentage of GDP declined by about one-
quarter from the mid-1970s to the mid-1990s. Together with our chron-
ically low private savings rate, government's large budgetary deficits
help drive the trade balance into the red. For the past three decades,
America's trade deficit has closely followed its combined (i.e., federal,

state, and local) governmental budgetary deficit. Since state and local government budgets consistently run sizable surpluses, it is the federal budget deficit that is most responsible for driving our combined public-private savings rate downward.

Another factor driving up the trade deficit in recent years has been rapidly rising foreign private investment in the U.S. Many foreigners choose to invest their savings in the United States because of its political stability and dynamic economy. From 1987 to 1996, for example, foreigners sank nearly a trillion dollars into U.S. securities and direct private investments.[17] Much of this inflow of foreign money went to pay for imported capital goods, which comprise by far the largest and most rapidly growing single category of this nation's imports. These capital imports help to build new factories and facilities.[18] In so doing, they help create jobs for American workers.

Rapid Economic Growth in Populous, Export-Oriented Developing Nations

A third key force shaping the American economy is economic development abroad, particularly in Asia, but also in Latin America. Today Asia is the most dynamic continent in terms of economic growth and trade expansion. The rapid growth of the Japanese economy beginning in the 1960s was followed a decade later by the emergence of four other swiftly growing, newly industrializing countries (NICs)—Hong Kong, Singapore, South Korea, and Taiwan. The collective GDP of these four NICs more than tripled between 1980 and 1994.[19]

More recently, China has achieved remarkable economic growth; in fact, since 1980 China's rate of GDP growth has exceeded that of the NICs. China has grown economically because it has shifted away from central economic planning; as a result, it now welcomes private investment from overseas and is moving gradually toward a more predictable, law-based economic system.

The Indian economy has also begun to expand, although less rapidly than China's and those of the NICs. India's economy, like China's, is now becoming less socialized, more hospitable to private investment. In

1994 its real GDP was nearly double the 1980 level. Other Asian nations, such as Thailand, Indonesia, Malaysia, and Vietnam, are also growing more quickly now.

Asia's Rapid Economic Growth is Likely to Continue for Many Years

Some economists have argued that there is nothing "miraculous" about East Asian economic growth; it simply results from pouring in more labor and capital.[20] These economists contend that other countries' rates of growth have declined as they exhausted their "reserves" of unproductively employed labor, and that Asian rates of growth must eventually decline as well.

These arguments, as far as they go, are correct. It is easy to acknowledge that there is nothing "miraculous" about Asian economic growth. It is easy also to acknowledge that most Asian countries have far to go in creating the institutional infrastructure they will need to sustain high levels of investment and growth.[21] So, while Asian rates of growth will eventually decline to levels typical of the world's already developed countries, demography suggests that "eventually" may be a long time coming.[22] That is so for two reasons: large labor reserves and export growth potential.

The Asian economic expansion is likely to continue for decades, because the labor "reserves" of the largest and most rapidly growing Asian countries will persist well into the twenty-first century. Their populations are huge, growing rapidly (at least in absolute terms), and still primarily rural. From 1980 to 1993, for example, China's population grew by 1.4 percent per year, with an impressive urban population growth rate of 4.3 percent per year. Still, only 29 percent of the Chinese population lived in cities in 1993, which means that urbanization will continue in the decades ahead.[23] As Asian populations urbanize, their economic productivity will continue to increase.

Moreover, as the Asian economies continue to grow, their manufacturing sectors will become increasingly important. In China, for example, manufacturing's share of GDP is now approximately 40 percent, up from less than 30 percent in 1970.[24] The same trend is evident in all

FIGURE 1-5
EXPORTS OUTPACE ECONOMIC GROWTH
IN ASIA'S RAPIDLY DEVELOPING ECONOMIES

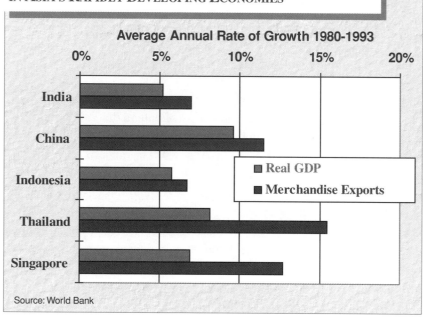

Source: World Bank

other developing Asian economies. In the advanced industrialized countries of the West, by contrast, manufacturing's share of GDP and employment has been declining for decades. These trends will continue into the next century.

The Asian economies will also become still more prominent exporters (see Figure 1-5). The Asian countries specialize in employing medium-level technologies to produce mass-manufactured goods for export; many of these goods are sold to the U.S. Asian countries have recently been extremely successful as exporters: South Korea's exports grew at an average annual rate of 22.7 percent from 1970 to 1980, and Hong Kong's grew by 15.8 percent per year from 1980 to 1993.[25] Now China and the other developing Asian economies are following the same path.

Asia has no monopoly on rapid growth led by exports of low- and medium-tech manufactured goods. Some Latin American countries,

Mexico notably among them, have set out on the same path trod by the Asian "tigers." Dozens of Mexican cities boom with the growth of *maquiladora* factories employing inexpensive labor to manufacture goods for the North American market. Typically, such goods are late in their technological life cycles and their production makes intensive use of low-skilled labor.

As the United States imports Asian and Latin American low- and medium-tech manufactured goods in ever greater quantities, the effect on our economy is threefold:

1. Consumers of clothing, footwear, electronic products, toys, and other mass-manufactured goods will purchase them at lower prices than they would have had to pay domestic producers. Thus all American consumers of these products save money when they buy them.
2. The market for goods and services exported by Americans grows, as buyers in developing countries increase their purchasing power. Since our highly competitive export industries tend to be our most productive and to pay high wages, their expansion produces more good jobs and raises American living standards.
3. Finally, Asian and Latin American exports successfully compete with the comparable goods produced by some American firms. As a result, the jobs of American workers who produce such goods will be at increasing risk.

Low-Skilled American Manufacturing Workers Face Increasing Direct Competition

Until recently America did not trade very much with the populous developing countries. Because that was so, few products from these countries were imported into America, which continued to produce goods that could have been made at lower cost by workers abroad. Thus there was no threat to the jobs and—by global standards—high earnings of modestly skilled American workers who produced such goods. Low-skilled American workers have enjoyed and still enjoy higher wages and higher living standards than their counterparts in other countries of the world.

This protracted protection from foreign competition perpetuated the unrealistic notion that Americans were somehow guaranteed a higher living standard than that of workers abroad who produced goods and services of equal or greater value. Today, however, globalization is eliminating that disparity. America now imports more goods from low-wage countries, and the high wages earned by unskilled American workers are no longer protected.

Why have America's low-skilled workers traditionally earned high wages by global standards? It is because they have been largely sheltered from the competition of similarly skilled foreign workers. Compared to the developing nations of Asia and Latin America, the United States has had a scarcity of unskilled labor and a relative surplus of well-educated, skilled workers. Within a protected domestic market, that relative scarcity translates into wages for unskilled workers that are high by global standards, relative to the wages of workers with better skills.

Figure 1-6 forcefully makes this point. It compares the average annual earnings (adjusted for the cost of living) of American workers in four different occupations with the earnings of their counterparts in five major cities of the developing world. Two of the occupations are skilled (those of skilled industrial workers and engineers), and the other two are moderately skilled or unskilled (those of construction workers and textile workers).

Close inspection reveals that American workers in all the occupations earn more than their counterparts in all the other cities surveyed. But the semiskilled and unskilled workers earn much more in America, relative to the highly skilled, than they do in the other cities. Thus American semiskilled or unskilled construction workers earn nearly ten times as much, on average, as their counterparts in the cities of the developing countries. Similarly, American unskilled textile workers earn nearly five times as much, on average, as unskilled textile workers in the other countries. Meanwhile, however, engineers earn only 2.6 times as much in America as elsewhere.

At least from the standpoint of labor costs, then, the United States has an international comparative advantage in goods produced by highly skilled workers, who are paid relatively less in this country than in the developing world. Conversely, the less developed countries have a comparative advantage in goods produced by low-skilled workers. Logically,

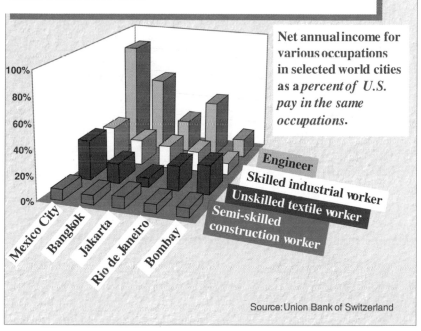

FIGURE 1-6
LOW-SKILLED WORKERS IN DEVELOPING COUNTRIES ARE
PAID LESS, RELATIVE TO THE HIGHLY SKILLED, THAN
THEY ARE IN THE U.S.

Net annual income for
various occupations
in selected world cities
as a *percent of U.S.
pay in the same
occupations.*

100%
80%
60%
40%
20%
0%

Engineer
Skilled industrial worker
Unskilled textile worker
Semi-skilled
construction worker

Mexico City
Bangkok
Jakarta
Rio de Janeiro
Bombay

Source: Union Bank of Switzerland

then, the United States should export goods in which it has the comparative advantage and import those in which it does not. That, in fact, is
exactly what tends to happen: we export goods like aircraft, software,
and computers, but we import clothing, shoes, toys, and consumer electronic products.

In short, America benefits greatly from its growing international
trade with the developing nations of Asia and elsewhere. All American
workers are able to buy less expensive goods, and highly skilled workers in the export sector earn more as world wide demand for their services
grows. The downside, though, is that poorly skilled workers here face
growing competition from their counterparts in the rapidly growing
nations of Asia and elsewhere in the developing world. The importation
of low-skills-intensive goods has the same effect on American labor

markets as an increase in the supply of low-skilled workers. When that happens, our relative scarcity of low-skilled labor decreases, because the low-skilled workers of the developing world are now producing goods for the American market.

Greater integration of the global economy in the early twenty-first century means that workers abroad will find their pay increasing; it will approach the compensation of comparable American workers. Their increased incomes and purchasing power will enlarge the market for American exports and the services of the workers who produce them.

On the other hand, unskilled Americans who produce goods that can be imported more cheaply will find their wages under downward pressure and their jobs increasingly at risk. Furthermore, workers displaced from jobs lost to import competition will increase the supply (and lower the wages) of unskilled workers seeking jobs in industries that do not themselves face direct competition from imports.

This force will tend to depress pay for unskilled workers throughout the economy. On the other hand, countervailing forces will push in the opposite direction later in this chapter: we will show that the aging of America and the success of our high-tech sector will spur demand for some sorts of unskilled labor. Exactly how the balance will be struck for America's unskilled workers remains unclear. Nevertheless, the surest road to better earnings is in having more knowledge and better skills.

Deregulation and Liberalization, Both Nationally and Globally

The fourth force affecting our economy is the continuing deregulation and liberalization of markets both here and abroad. Direct government interference in the economy has decreased, as have official barriers limiting the free play of market forces. While some nations have made greater progress than others, the trend toward greater economic freedom is global in scope.[26]

Economic liberalization means that there are fewer restrictions on international trade; freer convertibility of currencies; a greater reliance on private ownership as the spur to economic growth; increased acceptance of foreign investment; and expanded membership in global economic institutions such as the International Monetary Fund, the World Bank, and the World Trade Organization.

Arguably, economic liberalization has been most dramatic in the former communist nations. Beginning in 1978 (in China), 1989 (in eastern Europe), and 1991 (in the former USSR), the transition from centrally planned to market economies continues in nations whose combined population exceeds 1.6 billion people—nearly one-third of the world total. Private-property rights are being defined and strengthened. Ownership of state-owned enterprises and other property is being privatized. Prices are being decontrolled. Economies are being opened to foreign trade and foreign investment. Legal environments and other institutions are being revamped to support market economies.

Not surprisingly, given the great historical differences among the former communist nations, the transition from planned to market economies is proceeding quite unevenly; some nations are progressing more rapidly than others. And even the leaders will require decades to undo the damage wrought on their economies by forty to seventy years of communist rule. Still, the transition proceeds: huge areas that were formerly isolated from the global economy are joining the free-market system, introducing hundreds of thousands of new producers and millions of new consumers to the global market.

Because developing nations now understand that economic liberalization is the key to rapid growth, many of their economies are opening up as well. For example, Latin American nations from Mexico to Argentina are privatizing state holdings, stabilizing currencies, and dismantling protectionist trade barriers. Among the world's less developed regions, only Africa has yet to show much progress toward liberalization.

Economic freedom is increasing in the developed nations as well. The British economy, for example, has become much more dynamic in the wake of the reforms introduced by Margaret Thatcher. In the United States, deregulation has enabled market forces to play a larger role in many important industries, including the airlines, trucking, telecommunications, and banking.

World trade has also been encouraged, on both regional and global levels. Regionally, Europe's Economic Union is decreasing the barriers to trade among its member nations. Similarly, the North American Free Trade Association (NAFTA) is promoting trade among Canada, Mexico, and the U.S. And globally, more nations now adhere to the conditions of the World Trade Organization; as a result, barriers to international trade will continue to erode.

The effect of economic liberalization is to facilitate the movement of products, services, and capital within and among nations. That greater mobility brings greater competition in both product and labor markets.

Boomer Demographics: The Middle Aging of America

The four forces that we have discussed to this point are global in nature. The final force shaping our economy is a demographic one. At issue is the impact of the aging of the nearly 83 million Americans now living who were born in the two decades following the end of World War II. These so-called baby boomers are far more numerous than those born earlier or later. Forty-six percent fewer Americans now alive were born between 1926 and 1945; and 11 percent fewer were born between 1966 and 1985. The aging of this substantial cohort of post-World War II baby boomers will significantly affect America's economy.

Just as the baby boomers strained the capacity of the nation's elementary schools after 1950, they will fuel increased demand for elder-care facilities after 2010. Between now and then, their numbers and the growing volume of their purchasing power will create more demand for the goods and services that people choose in their later middle age. For example, they will consume more financial services as they save and invest more to provide for their retirement years.

Older Americans were becoming more common even before the boomers entered middle age. Better health care, diets, and lifestyles have been prolonging life expectancies for decades, resulting in a remarkable increase in the number of people living past age 70, 80, and even 90. The number of Americans age 75 and older jumped from 10 million in 1980 to 14.8 million in 1995, an increase of 48 percent. Meanwhile, the total population was growing by only 16 percent.[27] This surge in the older population, coupled with more generous financial support for retirement, has already increased demand for products and services desired by the elderly. The expansion of America's "Sunbelt" is traceable in large part to the growing numbers of the elderly. Medicare, the federally mandated system of health care for the elderly, has become far more costly as our population has aged; it faces financial insolvency early in the next century unless steps are taken soon to reform it.

But the geriatric surge we have seen up to now will pale in comparison to what the future will bring. Demand for goods and services tailored to the elderly will grow enormously. Because the spending patterns of older consumers tend largely to favor services, the demand for these services will skyrocket. That soaring demand will create millions of new jobs to be filled by workers who span the spectrum from highly skilled (e.g., registered nurses) to moderately skilled (e.g., repair personnel) to unskilled (e.g., home health aides).

Many of these jobs will involve manual labor, because aging boomers will be less inclined than they once were to do life's heavy lifting. And because many of the services required by older citizens must be delivered in person, the aging of the baby boomers will create many jobs in local communities they inhabit.

We discuss the economic impact of the aging boomers in more detail in Chapter 3. Let us now examine the ways in which the collective impact of our five forces will alter the American economy.

Broader Markets for Products, Services, and Capital

The mutually reinforcing influences of rapid technological change, globalization, Asian economic expansion, economic liberalization, and demographic change are transforming the American economy by expanding markets for countless goods and services, from soap to software to financial services. They are broadening the scope of these markets by bringing more actors—producers and consumers—into play. Faster and cheaper communications and transportation mean that companies that once catered to local or regional customers now face competition not only from firms in the same state or region but from across the nation and even around the globe. As a result, consumers now can choose from a wider range of similar products.

These forces are also rearranging markets in another way. By spawning new products and services and bringing old ones within convenient reach, they are dramatically increasing buyers' depth of choice. Markets now not only offer many similar products, but also a range of somewhat different ones that may provide more or less equal satisfaction to the buyer. Music lovers, for example, can satisfy their craving by attending a live concert, listening to a favorite radio station, or playing a video CD on a powerful stereo system that virtually recreates the concert-hall experience. Investors can fill their portfolios with an expanding array of financial instruments, from conventional stocks and bonds to mutual funds to derivatives.

In short, one type of product or service can increasingly be substituted for another. Markets are deepening by offering buyers much greater choice. Broader and deeper markets are a blessing to buyers, but a bane to producers who hope to corner a market.

Diminishing Monopoly and Intensifying Competition Everywhere

A second outcome of the forces discussed earlier is that monopolies are coming under attack. The protection once provided by geography and the unavailability of satisfactory substitutes is fast disappearing for more and more producers.

Consider what is happening in telecommunications. AT&T once virtually monopolized American telephony. Today, after divesting its local telephone providers in the 1980s, it faces stiff competition from Concert (the alliance between MCI and British Telecom), Sprint, and other providers of long-distance service. Now cable companies, wireless service providers, and the Internet offer an even wider range of choices. The combination of technological innovation and deregulation is destroying the vestiges of the telecommunications monopoly in America. That is good news for the American people and their economy; but it is bad news for those who benefited from the profits and security the old monopoly provided.

Other examples of diminishing monopoly and intensifying competition abound. IBM, which once dominated the computer market, is now just one of the players—an important one, to be sure, but shorn of the near-monopoly it once enjoyed. Similarly, the "Big Three" automobile producers lost their hammerlock on American car buyers in the 1980s.

Local banking offers another striking example. Not so long ago, Americans wishing to save or borrow money had to do business with banks in their local communities. But now, because of technological innovations and deregulation, local banks must compete not only with national and international banks but, increasingly, with other providers of financial services as well: money-market funds compete with bank certificates of deposit for local savings; credit-card companies compete for loans; and automatic teller machines (ATMs) compete to provide cash. The broadening and deepening of financial markets leave local bankers with no protection from competition, no shelter for easy profits or the easy life.

Large and small, local and national, "natural" and artificial, monopolies retreat as markets for goods and services broaden and deepen. Significantly, monopoly's last redoubt is the public sector, which grants monopoly power to certain governmental agencies. Thus first class mail can be sent only through the U.S. Postal Service; publicly funded education is available only from government-run schools. But even legally buttressed public monopolies like these are under increasing threat from companies like Federal Express and ideas like school choice.

How do former monopolies respond to increased competition? The short answer is that they either change or die. They wean themselves from the "rents" they enjoyed when they were protected from competition. They cut the fat and do more with less. They focus on what they do best and divest the rest. They learn to compete for profits.

AT&T may not especially welcome increased competition, but it is learning to live with it and even hoping to thrive in it. The same is true of IBM, the "Big Three" car makers, and every other erstwhile beneficiary of unusual market power in the private sector. Even Microsoft, which enjoys an unrivaled degree of market power today, fears that it may be displaced tomorrow. To be a successful competitor means being innovative, ready to change in response to market signals, and—above all—working constantly to give customers what they want. Companies that cannot compete will not survive.

In a competitive economy, businesses function as the agents of consumers. Businesses hire the services of capital and labor as inputs, and they combine them by using available technology to provide consumers with the goods and services they want. Consumers strive to gain the most satisfaction from the money they spend on goods and services; profits are what consumers pay businesses as their agents for helping them achieve that satisfaction. Good agents receive good payment; poor ones are paid accordingly.

Because companies face increasing competition, they must live with unrelenting pressure to become more efficient and to respond quickly to changing technological and market circumstances. They must give customers what they want at the lowest cost, or the customers will go elsewhere. Because this is so, the demise of monopoly is important for American workers.

Employers are obviously under greater pressure to keep costs— including labor costs—down when competition is keen than when some degree of monopoly power allows them to pass higher costs on to consumers in the form of higher prices or lower quality. That is why union bargaining is rarely successful when the employer sitting across the negotiating table does business in a highly competitive marketplace. In that case, there are no abnormally high profits to divide. This fact explains the decline of trade unions in America: workers are less likely to join unions if collective bargaining cannot raise their pay.

As America faces even stiffer competition in the twenty-first century, with monopoly in retreat throughout the private sector, labor unions are unlikely to rebound. Union prospects are better in the public sector, and will remain so as long as the force of law or regulation keeps competition there at bay.

Individual workers also are greatly affected by the decline of monopoly and intensifying competition throughout the economy. The competitive pressure exerted on employers translates directly into pressure on employees. Workers who give employers what they need to satisfy their customers will enjoy a huge advantage over those who do not—and will be paid accordingly. Every worker is, so to speak, the president and CEO of himself or herself. To survive and flourish in the twenty-first century, individual Americans will need to manage their most important assets—their workplace skills—with the same kind of attention and responsiveness to market signals characteristic of successful companies.

Booming Local Markets

The third change in the American economy will result in part from a demographic force. Local jobs in local communities are destined to grow rapidly in the early twenty-first century, as the baby boomers age. A second factor spurring this job growth will be the prosperity produced in communities that are participating in the economic expansion of America's high-tech sector.

The prosperity of any community hinges on its "export base" of specialized goods and services that are provided to customers in national and global markets. A strong export base creates wages, salaries, and profits in the pockets and bank accounts of those who produce the exports. Their purchasing power, in turn, creates higher demand for many locally provided goods and services. Rising incomes among computer engineers, financial managers, and lawyers ripple out into their communities whenever they make a purchase at a local store, eat at a restaurant, visit a chiropractor, hire an accountant, or engage a lawn-care specialist.

One well-known economist recently noted that most of the employment in America is in "activities, goods and (especially) services that are provided by local workers, to local consumers, for local consumption."[28] Retail salespersons, social workers, elementary school teachers, janitors—all provide services to local customers. Jobs like these are held by most people in most American communities. Few of these jobs are amenable to automation, and virtually none of them is directly vulnerable to competition from cheap foreign labor.

As a result, rapid technological progress and America's greater integration into the global economy are linked to the prosperity of local communities: increased productivity and the heightened success of our export industries will lead to payoffs on the local level.

It is encouraging to realize that demographic change and prosperity within communities will generate large numbers of jobs in the early twenty-first century. Most will be ordinary jobs requiring skills that are within the reach of most average Americans. But there is an important caveat: communities that do not participate in the expansion of America's growth sectors will also fail to reap these benefits.

The Continuing Shift of Production from Goods to Services

The fourth major change in the American economy will be in what we produce. At the beginning of the twentieth century, 63 percent of American workers produced goods, and only 37 percent produced services. Farming alone occupied more than 40 percent of the workforce in 1900; manufacturing accounted for another 13 percent. Americans mainly produced *things* in those days.[29]

But by 1970 the situation had already changed drastically. In that year, only some 30 percent of American workers produced goods. Farmers made up less than 5 percent of the workforce, and workers in manufacturing comprised 22 percent, down from the 1953 peak of 30 percent. By 1990, only 22 percent of the nation's total workforce produced goods, and 78 percent produced services. According to U.S. government projections, these trends will continue into the twenty-first century, though the shift away from goods production will decelerate. The Bureau of Economic Analysis estimates that 83 percent of the American workforce will be in the service sector by 2025.[30]

In fact, these impressive figures understate the shift in American employment toward white-collar work. Official data on employment by the industrial sector do not take into account the shift from physical to white-collar work *within* the goods-producing sectors. For example, from 1983 to 1993 the manufacturing sector lost 627,000 jobs. But Figure 1-7 shows that those cuts were distributed unevenly among the various major occupational categories. Physical production jobs (those held by operators, fabricators, laborers, etc.) did indeed decrease. But white-collar positions (those occupied by executives, other professionals, and marketers) actually increased in the manufacturing sector.[31]

When retirements are taken into account, all the net labor-force growth from now until 2020 will be in white-collar work. According to projections made by the Bureau of Economic Analysis, there will be

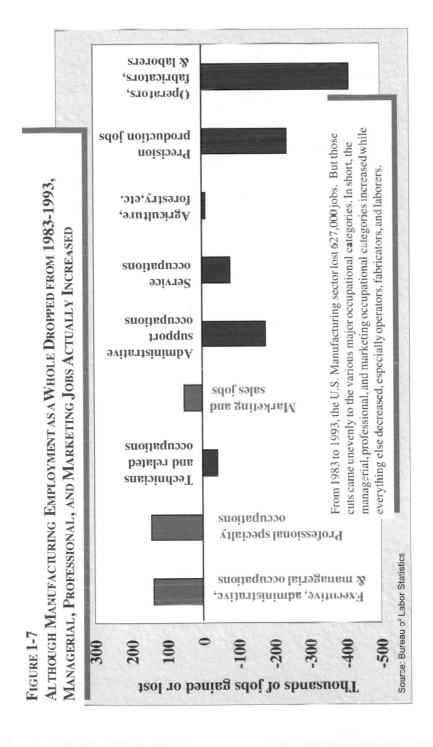

FIGURE 1-7

ALTHOUGH MANUFACTURING EMPLOYMENT AS A WHOLE DROPPED FROM 1983-1993, MANAGERIAL, PROFESSIONAL, AND MARKETING JOBS ACTUALLY INCREASED

From 1983 to 1993, the U.S. Manufacturing sector lost 627,000 jobs. But those cuts came unevenly to the various major occupational categories. In short, the managerial, professional, and marketing occupational categories increased while everything else decreased, especially operators, fabricators, and laborers.

Source: Bureau of Labor Statistics

only slightly more than 31 million people producing goods in 2020, about the same number as in 1990. The shift to services is even more pronounced when we look at individual occupations. Every one of the occupations expected to grow most rapidly between 1994 and 2005 is a service-type job, according to projections made by the Bureau of Labor Statistics.[32]

Information technology spurs service-sector growth. The service industries will be affected most dramatically by the IT revolution we discussed earlier. Improved computers and telecommunications facilitate electronic storage, transmission, and processing of vast quantities of information anywhere at any time. Thus by 2005 the Internet, intranets (proprietary networks similar to the Internet), and other networks will have transformed entire industries, such as financial services, banking, publishing, and retailing.

Technology is transforming the financial-services industry at an amazing rate. Approximately 1.5 million American investors already had on-line brokerage accounts by late 1996, nearly twice as many as expected only two years earlier.[33] The value of assets managed on-line is expected to quintuple to more than half a trillion dollars by 2001. On-line investing appeals not only to technological sophisticates but also to retirees and other ordinary investors eager to take advantage of its better and more timely information, greater convenience, and lower cost. On-line investing will revolutionize stock brokerage and other financial services as we have known them. No less significantly, it will broaden the horizons of ordinary investors to include more of the world's capital markets. As a result, these investors will be able to diversify their portfolios and take advantage of investment opportunities worldwide.

In banking, the technological revolution that began in the 1970s with ATMs will accelerate in the years ahead as on-line banking takes hold. A customer in Boston will find it as convenient to do business with a bank in Seattle—or Singapore—as with one a few blocks away. Huge savings in transactions costs await the pioneers in on-line banking. The technology will be implemented rapidly, because it will offer customer convenience and transaction efficiency.

No sector will be more thoroughly transformed by computer networks than retailing. Computers and telecommunications already make possible integrated point-of-sale and inventory-management systems. These highly sophisticated systems permit larger retail turnover with less costly (and less skilled) checkout personnel and with less money tied up in inventories. Just ahead lies interactive on-line shopping, which will provide many more alternatives to consumers, enabling them to compare prices and product features quickly and easily. On-line shopping will not replace conventional store-based retailing, but it will soon displace catalog shopping as the second most important form of retail distribution.

Electronic shopping will benefit customers, offering them more purchasing options and more reliable information. Shoppers will use network-based "intelligent agents" that have been "taught" individual buyers' preferences; they will be able to search and evaluate vendors' offerings on a nationwide or even global basis to find the best possible purchases.

Network interaction between buyers and vendors will enable retailers to make individually tailored products and deliver them directly to consumers. The traditional lag between product (or service) design and manufacture, on the one hand, and consumer choice, on the other, will be shortened and eventually eliminated. Whereas yesterday's technology dictated that most products had to be designed and produced before buyers could make their purchasing decisions, tomorrow's interactive technology will permit buyers to make their choices before the product is even manufactured. Better and more timely information about buyers' preferences will also allow vendors to identify which products are succeeding in the marketplace and to tailor production accordingly.

These new channels of distribution will gradually erode the market positions of many traditional retailers. At the same time they will open up opportunities for new providers of electronic shopping options. Unhindered by geography, retailers who employ the new technology will be able to sell to huge numbers of new customers without incurring the normally high costs of retail expansion—renting more space, increasing inventory, and hiring more workers.

Consumers armed with PCs and credit cards will be able to shop at stores anywhere in the world. As large numbers of the world's consumers begin on-line global searching for the best deal possible, American retailers will enjoy major competitive advantages. Their skills honed by decades of competitive struggle at home, American retailers are already the world's low-cost providers.

Publishing will also witness major changes induced by technology in the years ahead. Electronic distribution of journals, magazines, and newspapers is rapidly becoming commonplace. Low costs of entry will encourage innovators to launch new publishing ventures designed to exploit the Internet's main advantages: global readership; multimedia combinations of text, audio, and video information; and—most of all—interactivity. But printed publications will not simply vanish into cyberspace: newspapers and magazines that adapt to the new reality will survive the impact of electronic publishing, just as they have survived the onslaught of television. Indeed, electronic publishing, with its added demand for novel content and design, is likely to create many new opportunities for journalists, while destroying relatively few old ones.

These examples, coupled with our earlier discussion of the IT industries, illustrate critical features of America's emerging high-tech, globalized economy:

- Ever-shorter product cycles will compress the time from a product's conceptualization through design, manufacture, and distribution. New products will appear, reach maturity, and become obsolete in rapid succession.
- Prices will be set low, as producers strive to gain early market share and define industry standards for their wares.
- A premium will be placed on rapidity and responsiveness in product design, engineering, and marketing.
- Management structures and personnel responsibilities will change frequently, as businesses rush to keep pace. Adaptability and agility will be the new keys to survival.

Summary: Implications for the American Workforce

To be a productive worker in America's fast-paced, rapidly changing, technology-driven, globally competitive economy is not, nor will it be, easy. Our analysis of the economic forces at work points to the following conclusions:

- Wages and salaries will be under constant pressure. By no means will compensation sink for all workers. Far from it; many workers will find that growing demand for their skills and knowledge brings heftier paychecks. But employers in highly competitive markets will be unable to pay their workers more than the value of what they produce. Pay will increasingly be linked to performance.
- Workers will change jobs more often. Rapid change dictated by competitive pressures will force companies to evaluate their staffing needs constantly, which will lead to frequent "re-sizing" of their workforces. As a result, workers will change jobs, employers, and even occupations more often than in the past. Moreover, workers in all occupations will need to prepare themselves mentally and professionally for this uncertainty.
- Labor unions will face more difficult times. A more competitive, rapidly changing entrepreneurial economy, in which smaller firms account for a larger share of production and employment, is an inhospitable environment for unions. The percentage of American workers who are union members is therefore likely to continue its gradual decline.
- America's swiftly developing technologies will increase the demand for highly skilled and well-educated workers. A rapidly changing and more entrepreneurial economy places a premium on both adaptability and flexibility; workers able to master technology and cope with change will have an advantage.
- Unskilled and poorly educated workers will face multiple threats in tomorrow's labor markets. Modern technology—especially IT— tends to reduce the demand for unskilled labor. Globalization will increase U.S. consumption of imported goods and services produced by low-skilled workers. As a result, there will be less demand for low-skilled workers who produce comparable goods and services here. A rapidly changing economy will harm low-skilled and poorly educated workers who cannot adapt to changes in the workplace.
- Offsetting these reductions in the demand for unskilled workers will be expanding demand for local services, many of them produced by workers with only low or modest skills. In addition, the aging of the baby boomers, combined with general prosperity, will greatly

stimulate local demand for personal services the provision of which requires few skills and not much education.

- In the long run, the difficulties faced by low-skilled workers may recede. In time, technological innovation and capital investment will once again increase the demand for low-skilled labor (as they did when assembly-line production began), especially if highly skilled labor becomes prohibitively expensive. Furthermore, rising wages for unskilled workers in the developing countries will eventually reduce their comparative advantage in the production of low-tech goods, thereby relieving import-generated downward pressure on the jobs and wages of low-skilled American workers. But many years will elapse before these developments occur, years in which low-skilled American workers will face increasing economic difficulties. Low-skilled workers—as well as all other Americans—will therefore benefit if we upgrade skills throughout the workforce, enabling more workers to fill the good jobs certain to be available.

CHAPTER TWO
CHANGES IN WORK, COMPENSATION, AND OCCUPATIONS

We begin this chapter by explaining how and why the nature of work is changing as America enters the twenty-first century. Here we elaborate on the workforce implications of the changes in the American economy discussed in Chapter 1, examining the growing irrelevance of gender in the workplace, the extent to which job security is decreasing, the increase in temporary employment, and the shift away from work in traditional offices made possible by "telecommuting." We then explore alterations in American earning patterns. In this section we look at the distribution of earnings; the changes in individuals' earnings levels over time that demonstrate income mobility; the earnings patterns of whites, blacks, and Hispanics; and the correlation between educational attainment and earnings. Finally, we consider changes in occupational structure that are now emerging. Here we explore the overall growth to come in American employment, the specific occupations that will expand and contract, and the skill levels tomorrow's jobs will require.

The Changing Nature of Work

Globalization and technological innovations are rapidly changing the nature of America's work and workplaces. These changes, in turn, profoundly affect who is doing work and how and where it is carried out.

Gender Shift in the Workplace

Early in the twentieth century biology was destiny in the American workplace. With few exceptions, the work to be done was more easily performed by men than by women. But that is emphatically no longer the case. Now that the nature of work has changed, almost all jobs today can be done as easily by women as by men. This gender shift may be the most significant change in the history of the American workplace.

A century ago, the American workplace was predominantly a place in which men produced agricultural and manufactured goods. Most women worked as homemakers. To be sure, some women worked in gender-specific jobs as teachers and nurses, and others held bottom-end jobs in mills and sweatshops, or as domestics. A few women were also employed in various professions. All of these cases, though, were exceptions to the rule that the workplace was chiefly a masculine domain.

The farm and factory work of 1900 demanded plenty of brawn and relatively little brainpower. Back then, men were needed for the long hours of hard physical labor that defined most jobs. Formal schooling was required for few occupations, and most skills were learned on the job.

But as the 20th Century progressed, the nature of work changed, particularly after mid-century. As we have seen, the American economy has largely shifted from producing goods to providing services. At the same time, machines have increasingly substituted for manual labor in agriculture and industry. Thus brawn gradually lost its importance in the workplace.

As physical strength and other gender-specific traits came to be less important workplace attributes, more jobs could be held by women as well as men. The defense industry made this clear during World War II: men went off to war, and factory work was increasingly done by women. Since then, one gender barrier after another has toppled, and millions of American women have entered the workforce in the second half of the century. Today, of course, women are employed throughout the economy, producing goods and services alike.

Gender is particularly irrelevant in the service sector, which will employ the overwhelming majority of Americans in the early twenty-first century. In fact, if occupationally relevant gender differences exist today, they are as likely to favor women as men. Thus women seem to be preparing themselves more assiduously than men for professional careers in the information age: women now garner 55 percent of bachelor's degrees, 53 percent of master's degrees, and nearly 40 percent of doctorates.[1]

A trend of great importance is now emerging: in the decades ahead, men will lose whatever workplace advantage they may still retain. Increasingly, men are no longer the sole or even the primary sources of income for families. Already by 1993, wives were the sole earners in 20 percent of American married-couple families. That was up from 14 percent in 1980 and appears to be headed higher. Two-earner families, where both husband and wife were the family breadwinners, increased from 39 percent to 55 percent of all married-couple families over the same time period, a trend that also seems likely to persist.[2] Finally, women are the sole earners in nearly two-thirds of families maintained by a single person, a category that increased from 12 percent of all families in 1980 to 16 percent in 1993.

By 1997, nearly 60 percent of American women were already in the labor force, up from only 33 percent in 1950. Meanwhile, the share of American men in the labor force had dropped from 88 to 75 percent since 1950. Women now account for about 46 percent of the workforce, up from only 29 percent in 1950; in the years immediately ahead, they will approach parity with men.[3]

Increasing numbers of mothers of young children now hold jobs: approximately 64 percent of all married women with children under six years of age are in the workforce today. Only 18.6 percent of their counterparts were in the workforce in 1960; as recently as 1985 the figure stood at only 53.4 percent.[4]

This development has obvious and important implications for the American workplace. The mix of desired benefits and work conditions will change: flexible hours, telecommuting, and family leave will become increasingly attractive to both men and women who are parents of young children. In the early twenty-first century, employers who wish to recruit and retain highly skilled and well-educated workers will need to offer their employees benefits and working conditions such as these.[5]

Dynamic Labor Markets

In Chapter 1 we noted that companies must constantly innovate if they are to survive in an increasingly competitive marketplace. Today's firms can succeed and fail with astonishing rapidity, depending on how well they satisfy their customers.

Businesses that expand and contract quickly will be equally quick to hire and discharge employees. The result will be dynamic labor markets, as workers change jobs frequently. The phenomenon of "permanent" employment within a single firm is now almost an anachronism: for the most part, tomorrow's workers will no longer stay with the same firm throughout their working lifetimes.

The new reality, already increasingly apparent, is that most of us will change our employers and even our occupations several times in the course of our working lives. Individual workers must prepare themselves and their families to cope with the new reality, perhaps even to welcome it.

The uncertainty provoked by layoffs and "downsizing" has led many people to worry that employment in America is growing more tenuous and less stable, that workers are more frequently tossed about from job to job, and that part-time and temporary work are fast becoming the norm in American workplaces. The mass media have devoted great attention to corporate downsizing in the 1990s.[6] Some politicians have also voiced serious concern.[7] One would therefore suppose that lengthy job tenure is becoming a thing of the past. How valid is this concern? Will job security disappear early in the next century?

Contingent and Alternative Work Arrangements

Let us begin by examining what has happened in the recent past. The available data tell a story that is more complicated than—and often contradictory to—the one reported by the media. Consider, for example, the notion that job tenure[8] is declining sharply for all workers. In fact, there are important disparities in job tenure that are largely overlooked but which indicate a much more nuanced reality than is generally understood. More than anything else, these disparities reflect the changing composition of the workforce and the changing structure of the economy.

Overall, the median job tenure for male workers in 1996 was 4.0 years, virtually unchanged from what it was in 1983.[9] For women, overall median job tenure rose from 3.1 years to 3.5 during the same period; most of the increase came after 1990. Despite this overall stability, the growing frequency of job shifts and career changes becomes evident when job tenure data are examined at a finer level of detail. Looking at median job tenure *within* ten-year age brackets, we see tenure dropping for men of all ages. Those aged 55 to 64, for example, saw their job tenure fall from 15.3 years to 10.5 years between 1983 and 1996.

It is important to realize, though, that all workers have greater success in keeping jobs if they are better educated. For example, men without a high school diploma saw their job tenure drop by nearly one-third between 1983 and 1991, whereas the tenure of men with four or more years of college increased by 9 percent.[10]

The transformation of the American economy from goods production to service production has much to do with changing overall measures of job tenure. The service sector traditionally has shorter job tenure than manufacturing, mining, and transportation. Even though average job tenure in services is increasing, it remains considerably less than in these other industries. What is happening, then, is that more Americans are now working in a sector of the economy that tends to have shorter job tenure. For that reason alone, overall median job tenure is declining; significantly, though, job tenure within almost all individual sectors of the economy is actually increasing.

How many employed Americans are actually at risk of losing their jobs? Until recently, little was known about the size and nature of the "contingent workforce," as the Bureau of Labor Statistics infelicitously labels workers without an explicit or implicit contract for long-term employment. In fact, the contingent workforce was not measured rigorously until February 1995. That first assessment showed that contingent workers are both fewer in number and more heterogeneous than widely supposed.

Wage and salary workers who had been on the job for one year or less and expected that their jobs would last no more than one additional year comprised only 2.2 percent of the total employed workforce. When the self-employed and independent contractors were included, the share of contingent workers increased to 2.8 percent; when workers who had been on the job for more than one year were included, the share of workers expecting to lose their jobs in a year increased to 4.9 percent of total employment.[11] In short, even according to the broadest definition, workers who consider themselves likely to lose their jobs comprise less than 5 percent of all jobholders.[12]

Although their numbers are relatively small, contingent workers differ from the regularly employed in significant respects. The percentage of contingent workers who are young and in entry-level jobs is much larger. Women and minorities are also represented in somewhat greater proportions among contingent workers.

But contrary to what might be expected, the occupational category of "professional and specialty workers" supplies 20 percent of all contingent workers, compared with less than 15 percent of all non-contingent workers. The service sector employs well over half of all contingent workers but only about a third of the others. The proportion of workers without a high school diploma is some 70 percent higher among contingent workers narrowly defined (wage and salary workers only) than in the regularly employed workforce. When the definition of contingent worker is expanded to include the self-employed and independent contractors, however, workers with advanced degrees turn out to be more than proportionately represented (by nearly 40 percent).

In short, contingent workers are a very heterogeneous lot. Nearly 30 percent of them are well-educated professional workers, a majority of whom seem to prefer the flexibility of contingency to the relatively rigid requirements of regular employment. As a whole, contingent workers are not less well educated or less skilled than regularly employed workers. Surprisingly, about two-thirds of them have health insurance. Finally, about a third of all contingent workers claim to prefer their contingent status to conventional employment.[13]

Another cause of widespread concern is the growth of temporary work.[14] Should it be? The "indirect and alternative workforce," which is how the Bureau of Labor Statistics characterizes temporary workers, included nearly ten million individuals in February 1995.[15] More than two-thirds of these were classified as "independent contractors," of whom the vast majority (over 82 percent) expressed a preference for their "indirect or alternative" arrangement over conventional employment. Furthermore, a substantial majority of on-call workers (58 percent) and workers placed by temporary-help agencies (63 percent) preferred their "indirect or alternative" arrangement.

Fragmentary data suggest that the number of workers with indirect or alternative job arrangements was increasing briskly during the early 1990s.[16] American companies reportedly spent twice as much on temporary help in 1995 as they did only four years earlier.[17] That implies an average annual rate of increase of nearly 19 percent. But in the late 1990s this rapid growth seems to be slowing: the nation's temporary-help payroll grew by only 8.3 percent in the first quarter of 1996 compared to its level in the same period in 1995.[18] Even if it grew by half that rate until 2020, however, this nontraditional workplace arrangement could occupy as much as a quarter of the entire employed labor force at that time.

Nor should this increase be lamented. Not only does it provide flexible work arrangements to both employers and workers, it has other advantages as well. Many companies have discovered that hiring temporary workers is an efficient recruitment device; it allows them to "test drive" potential new employees far more effectively than by interviewing them. For their part, many job hunters have discovered that "temping" permits them to explore working for a potential long-term employer and to display their capacity to do a job well. Nearly 40 percent of temporary workers report that they have been offered full-time employment.[19]

This coincidence of interests suggests that workers in the various nontraditional work arrangements will become far more common in the years ahead. So far, they comprise a fairly small proportion of the total workforce—perhaps 10 percent of it. But as noted earlier, they may make up as much as 25 percent of the employed workforce by 2020. And if they resemble the profile of their 1995 predecessors, most of these workers will have chosen a nontraditional arrangement as a preferred alternative.

Telecommuting

High-speed, reliable telecommunications devices open up new options for many workers. Rapid advances in telecommunications in the

1980s allowed increasing numbers of American workers to work out-side a traditional office setting, mostly at home. "Telecommuting"—using telecommunications technology to do work without commuting to an office—is becoming increasingly common. We believe that tele-commuting will become even more common among the twenty-first century workforce, particularly given the need for highly skilled work-ers, as discussed below.

The U.S. Department of Transportation (DOT) estimates that in 1992 two million workers (1.6 percent of the labor force) telecommuted an average of one to two days per week.[20] The DOT predicts that the number of telecommuters may increase to fifteen million workers, rep-resenting over 10 percent of the workforce, by 2002. Other forecasts put the number closer to 25 million telecommuters by 2002.[21] A private research organization estimates that well over seven million people already telecommuted in 1994—and that the number of telecommuters is growing at 15 percent per year.[22]

As telecommunications advances become even more integrated into the American economy, we believe that telecommuting will become increasingly attractive to both employers and employees. Employers can cut corporate real estate costs and—as recent studies suggest—increase worker productivity by up to 20 percent.[23]

The Congressional Office of Technology Assessment identified three categories of jobs most appropriate for telecommuting: routine information-handling tasks, mobile activities, and professional and other knowledge-related tasks.[24] Telecommuting will be attractive to many workers in these jobs, because it will provide more flexible work arrangements. With the availability of reliable, high-speed telecom-munications networks, white-collar professionals—whose numbers, we shall see below, are slated to grow rapidly—will increasingly be able to take advantage of flexible work arrangements. That flexibility will particularly appeal—as we explain in the next chapter—to work-ers with young children and older workers, who may be more inclined to keep working if they can do so without commuting to an office every day.

What Has Happened to Earnings?

Growing Dispersion of Earnings

In 1983, approximately one quarter of all American workers were in the three highest-paying broad occupational categories (employed as executives, professionals, or technicians); by 1994 that figure had grown to 27 percent, and it is projected to reach approximately 30 percent by 2005.[25] Simultaneously, the share of all workers in the three lowest-paying categories (primarily in sales and service), which remained stable from 1983 to 1995 at about 29 percent, is predicted to reach 31 percent in 2005. In short, larger shares of workers will be found at both ends of the income distribution. The good news here is that the best-paying occupations are expanding more rapidly.

Proportionately fewer workers, though, are employed in the middle-paying occupations. Such workers made up 44 percent of the total in 1983. The figure fell to 40 percent in 1994, and the Bureau of Labor Statistics projects that it will decline to 39 percent in 2005.

These statistics show that the American economy has, on average, been creating better jobs overall. The change is measured by an Index of Job Quality (IJQ) devised by Hudson Institute, which explores the impact of the creation and disappearance of different sorts of jobs.[26] According to the IJQ, the overall quality of American jobs has been increasing by approximately 0.1 percent annually since 1983; if Bureau of Labor Statistics projections prove accurate, it will continue to improve at about the same rate through the year 2005.

Nevertheless, it is important to understand that the improvement of the "average" American job is actually the end product of forces pulling in opposite directions: the best-paying jobs are growing most rapidly (or else the average would not have improved), but the lowest-paying jobs are growing as well. Fewer jobs, as noted earlier, are found in the middle range.

In short, more American workers now are paid very well, and more are now paid comparatively poorly. In addition, highly paid workers today are increasing their income much more rapidly than poorly paid ones.[27]

The rapid increase in the number of well-paid American workers, coupled with the increasing remuneration offered by their jobs, is cause for celebration. Conversely, the increasing number of low-paid workers presents cause for concern—particularly when we note that their income is falling ever-farther behind the income of better-paid workers.

To summarize:

- An increasingly large percentage of American workers now benefits from higher living standards made possible by our increasingly globalized and technologically innovative economy.
- At the same time, a large but more slowly growing share of the workforce is gravitating toward sales and service positions that pay poorly by comparison.
- Proportionately fewer jobholders are found now in the middle-paying occupations. The income of moderately paid workers is rising far more rapidly than that of poorly paid workers; but the income of the best-paid workers is rising fastest of all.

These developments are all explained by the changes in the American economy discussed in Chapter 1. Technological advances mean that improved machines can increasingly substitute for unskilled and poorly educated human labor. Meanwhile, demand increases for workers equipped with the knowledge and skills required to employ the new technologies. There are and will continue to be jobs for unskilled workers: but they are unlikely to pay well enough to enable many of them to maintain the living standards they enjoyed in the past.

Income Mobility

Static "snapshots" of income distribution at a particular moment in time cause many to worry that economic inequality is rising in America. But too much is made of these findings, because people's incomes are not static but dynamic—that is, they change over time. A static picture of income distribution is of limited value: by definition, after all, any distribution must always include a top and a bottom 20 percent—or quintile—of earners.

Nevertheless, the concern about rising inequality seems to be buttressed by long-term data examining income distribution during a twenty-five-year period. Data from the Current Population Survey (CPS) for the years 1968 to 1992 suggest that certain groups are concentrated in the bottom of the earnings distribution. According to the CPS survey, women are more likely to be found in the lowest quintile of the overall earnings distribution than are men; blacks are more likely than whites to slip out of the top quintile; and people who are young, less educated, or black tend to have earnings that fluctuate more than the earnings of those who are older, better educated, or white.[28]

Even the CPS data are of limited value, though, because they ignore changes in *individuals'* income over time. That is to say, the particular individuals who made up 1968's bottom income quintile are not necessarily those found in 1992's bottom income quintile. Specifically, to the considerable extent that youth correlates with low earnings, it is important to realize that those who were young (and had low earnings) in 1968 were certainly older (and almost certainly had much higher earnings) by 1992. Thus the real question is whether the particular individuals and families in the top and bottom income groups change over time. In other words, how mobile is the distribution of American income?

Two different sets of data—from the University of Michigan's Panel Survey on Income Dynamics (PSID) from 1975 to 1991 and a U.S. Treasury Department database of income-tax returns from 1979 to 1988—enable us to answer that question, because they track the incomes of particular Americans over time. Their portrait of the distribution of American income is far more optimistic than that drawn by the CPS data, because they show that in fact income is extremely mobile: many people who were poor in earlier years become much wealthier later on.

Relying on data from these two sources, two economists with the Federal Reserve Bank of Dallas argue that low-income workers with basic skills, education, and the willingness to work tend to increase their earnings rapidly.[29] They report that according to the PSID, only 5 percent of the individuals in the bottom quintile of the income distribution in 1975 were still there in 1991. Furthermore, a majority of those who had been in the bottom quintile actually rose to places in the top three quintiles of the income distribution during this 16-year span. And for those Americans with more education and better skills, the rise in income is very rapid. Young, college-educated workers in 1975, for example, saw their real income increase fivefold by 1991.[30]

Data from the U.S. Treasury Department supports the PSID's key findings. As the Dallas Federal Reserve economists note, in the Treasury study 86 percent of those in the lowest income bracket in 1979 moved up to a higher bracket within nine years. Two-thirds of these Americans moved into the top three quintiles, and 15 percent of them moved all the way up into the top quintile of earners.[31]

Because of rapid technological change, further global integration, and increased competition, the American economy of the early twenty-first century will be an increasingly turbulent place to work. But American workers will still be able to increase their earnings significantly. Both the PSID and the Treasury data indicate that even the poorest Americans today can still achieve prosperity in the years ahead.

Skills and Education Strongly Influence Earnings

The impact of education is underscored by Figure 2-1, which shows how inflation-adjusted earnings of workers with various levels of education changed between 1975 and 1994.[32]

When data on average annual earnings are adjusted for inflation, they show that only workers with at least a high school diploma have actually gained ground. Workers with advanced and bachelor's degrees have, on average, considerably outdistanced those without a college degree. High school graduates saw their earnings increase marginally, and high school dropouts failed even to keep up with inflation.

Relative to high school graduates, college graduates and advanced-degree holders have improved their lot substantially since 1975. Median earnings for workers with advanced degrees increased steadily: in 1975 such workers earned 213 percent of the pay of workers who were high school graduates with no more than a high school diploma, but the figure rose to 277 percent in 1994. In 1972 workers with bachelor's degrees earned 57 percent more than high school graduates; but by 1994 they enjoyed an 84-percent advantage.

Figure 2-1
On Average, Better Educated Workers Earn Better

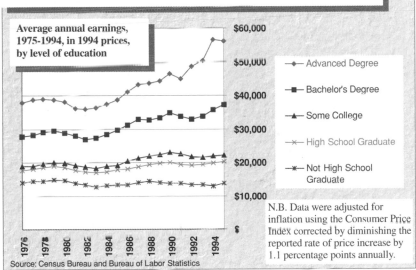

Average annual earnings, 1975-1994, in 1994 prices, by level of education

- Advanced Degree
- Bachelor's Degree
- Some College
- High School Graduate
- Not High School Graduate

N.B. Data were adjusted for inflation using the Consumer Price Index corrected by diminishing the reported rate of price increase by 1.1 percentage points annually.

Source: Census Bureau and Bureau of Labor Statistics

The Earnings of Whites, Blacks, and Hispanics

Another way to understand what has happened to wages is to examine trends among different segments of the population, particularly to see how education and occupational choice affect the wages of different groups. During the period 1987-1995, blacks' median earnings remained stable at about 75 percent of those of whites.[33] Asians' earnings declined slightly, from 98 to 96 percent of whites', over the same period. But Hispanics' earnings declined sharply both absolutely and relatively; their median earnings fell from 70 percent of whites' in 1987 to 64 percent in 1995.

This divergence between the earnings patterns of blacks and Hispanics raises grave doubts about the common assumption that these two populations can be grouped together as though they invariably share the same fate. The disparity in earnings between blacks and Hispanics also points to the key explanation of income patterns for *all* groups: divergent levels of education and skills.

The importance of education accounts for the overall failure of Hispanics to make significant gains in earnings. Unfortunately, the educational gains of Hispanics in the workforce pale in comparison to those made by whites and blacks. Note, for example, that one-third of the net additional Hispanic workers between 1975 and 1994 were high-school dropouts. By contrast, none of the net additional workers in the white and black cohorts had less than a high school diploma. The number of working white high school dropouts declined by 7.5 million (37 percent) between 1975 and 1994; the decline for blacks stood at 42 percent. But the number of working Hispanic high school dropouts increased by a remarkable (and troublesome) 31 percent.

These sharply rising numbers of Hispanics without a completed high school education are explained mainly by the large number of poorly educated Mexican immigrants now resident in this country. In 1994, more than 71 percent of the 4.2 million Mexican-born residents of the United States aged 25 years or older had not completed high school.[34] Since Mexican immigrants comprise about 60 percent of all foreign-born Hispanics (and 30 percent of *all* Hispanics) aged 25 years and older who resided in the United States in 1994, their contribution to Hispanics' overall low educational attainment is very substantial.[35]

Unfortunately, the educational deficit of Mexican immigrants is not confined to adults. Recent research indicates that a quarter of Mexican immigrants aged 15-17 were not in school—a level nearly 20 percent beneath that of any other immigrant group and 17 percent beneath that of U.S.-born youngsters of Mexican origin in the same age group.[36] Mexican-born immigrants are not so much dropping out of high school after they arrive in the United States as failing to "drop into" high school in Mexico before they immigrate.

Many of the occupational shifts that have taken place over the last twenty years have affected all three groups: whites, blacks, and Hispanics. The share of employment in executive and managerial positions grew for all groups. So, too, did the proportion of jobs in sales. Administrative-support positions became less common for whites, blacks, and Hispanics. Nonetheless, major differences among the groups do exist.

The first difference involves service occupations. The predominance of service employment diminished between 1986 and 1996 for whites and blacks; it increased, though, for Hispanics. Conversely, employment in the precision-production and craft occupations was more common for whites and blacks in 1996 than it had been in 1986; but the opposite was true for Hispanics.

And even within the occupations in which all groups experienced the same trend, the strength of the trend often differed significantly. The increase in the share of employment in executive and managerial positions was smaller for Hispanics than for whites or blacks. The decrease in administrative-support employment was also the smallest for Hispanics.

Thus the differing rates of change in average earnings over the last few decades have their root not only in differing levels of educational attainment but also in the occupational choices educational attainment make possible. The relatively modest educational gains of Hispanics have prevented them from being hired to fill many good jobs. As a result, their earnings have grown more slowly than those of whites and blacks.

The relationship between education and occupational choice also tells us much about future earnings for various groups. The Bureau of Labor Statistics predicts that nearly 4 percent of all job openings between 1994 and 2005 will require a postgraduate degree. By 1993 more than 4 percent of whites had attained such degrees; but less than 4 percent of blacks and Hispanics had. A greater proportion of whites will also be available to fill the jobs requiring bachelor's, associate's, or vocational degrees. Unless proportionately more blacks and—especially—Hispanics achieve better educations, their earnings cannot approach the level of whites' earnings.

In summary, the disparity between the earnings of workers who are more and less well-educated has grown. Holders of advanced degrees now earn more relative to workers with bachelor's degrees; at the same time, those with bachelor's degrees have lengthened their advantage over workers with some college education, and workers with some college education but no degree do marginally better than high school graduates. High school dropouts, to repeat, have seen their earnings decline both absolutely and relative to those of everyone else.

All available evidence indicates that these trends will continue at least into the first decade of the twenty-first century. These increasing disparities indicate that our economy now has a growing glut of un-skilled workers relative to the number of well-paying job opportunities for them—but also a growing relative scarcity of better-educated, highly skilled workers.

Higher Education is No Guarantee of Higher Earnings

The findings presented here unquestionably show a positive correlation between workers' earnings and their level of education. Still, it is wrong to believe—as many people do—that a college degree in any subject whatsoever is by itself a virtual guarantee of higher earnings.

Why is it wrong to believe that all college degrees produce higher earnings? First, correlation should not be confused with causation. It is true that average earnings rise with levels of formal education; but that does not prove that more education *causes* higher earnings. Instead, more education and higher earnings might both be caused by some additional factor or factors. For example, both are probably associated with attributes such as higher intelligence, greater personal discipline and ambition, favorable cultural and parental influences, etc. In short, it is likely that workers with such attributes would perform better and earn more than those without them, regardless of the levels of formal education received. Workers with these attributes may possess more formal education; but conceivably they would have obtained the skills and knowledge necessary to prosper even without formal education.

In addition, aggregate data on the earnings of college-educated workers obscure important differences among their incomes. The earnings of college-educated workers are better understood when we realize that they tend to earn very different sums depending on their fields of study.

Thus research shows that workers with recent degrees in engineering, the health sciences, computer and information sciences, and the physical sciences tend to earn much more than those with degrees in education, psychology, and the humanities. That conclusion is borne out by a comprehensive study of more than 12 million workers that considered major field of baccalaureate study, gender, occupation, and age. Tables 2-1a and 2-1b shows that earnings vary widely among and within the subjects studied.

Major field of study greatly affects earnings for all graduates in every age group (although only those aged 35-44 are shown in the two parts of Table 2-1). For both men and women, engineering, pharmacy, and

TABLE 2-1A (MEN)
PERCENT DISTRIBUTION OF EMPLOYMENT OF BACHELOR'S DEGREE HOLDERS, MALES AGED 35-44, BY EARNINGS QUINTILE AND MAJOR FIELD OF STUDY, 1993

Major field of study	Median annual earnings	Percent with annual earnings--				
		Greater than $62,400	From $49,001 to $62,400	From $39,001 to $49,000	From $30,001 to $39,000	Of $30,000 or less
All major fields of study	$ 43,199	19.9	20.0	19.4	17.6	23.1
Top five fields for men						
Engineering	$ 53,286	28.8	34.3	17.9	9.9	9.1
Mathematics	$ 51,584	27.9	28.0	15.8	15.3	13.0
Computer and information sciences	$ 50,509	23.4	30.9	25.0	12.5	8.2
Pharmacy	$ 50,480	11.1	47.2	26.8	7.9	7.0
Physics	$ 50,128	28.3	26.0	19.0	14.6	12.1
Bottom five fields for men						
Education	$ 34,470	8.5	11.1	18.6	24.5	37.3
Linguistics & foreign languages	$ 33,780	4.9	11.2	13.3	31.1	39.5
Visual and performing arts	$ 32,972	12.2	11.9	14.0	19.0	42.9
Social work	$ 32,171	3.7	17.5	16.7	18.9	43.2
Philosophy, religion, and theology	$ 31,848	11.5	7.2	15.4	18.8	47.1

Source: *Monthly Labor Review*, December 1995

TABLE 2-1B (WOMEN)
PERCENT DISTRIBUTION OF EMPLOYMENT OF BACHELOR'S DEGREE HOLDERS, *FEMALES* AGED 35-44,
BY EARNINGS QUINTILE AND MAJOR FIELD OF STUDY, 1993

Major field of study	Median annual earnings	Percent with annual earnings--				
		Greater than $47,000	From $36,001 to $47,000	From $29,642 to $36,000	From $25,551 to $29,541	Of $22,500 or less
All major fields of study	$ 32,155	19.9	19.2	20.9	20.0	20.0
Top five fields for women						
Economics	$ 49,170	53.9	8.6	15.0	5.3	17.2
Engineering	$ 49,070	56.5	18.1	10.2	7.8	7.4
Pharmacy	$ 48,427	62.1	23.4	6.7	1.2	6.6
Architecture/environmental design	$ 46,343	50.2	19.1	10.4	9.7	10.6
Computer and information sciences	$ 43,757	41.2	28.8	16.0	10.1	3.9
Bottom five fields for women						
Agriculture	$ 28,751	18.0	7.6	20.6	22.0	31.8
Social work	$ 28,594	10.1	12.6	24.3	29.1	23.9
Home economics	$ 28,275	9.8	13.8	20.2	27.6	28.6
Education	$ 27,988	8.3	13.8	22.4	27.3	28.2
Philosophy, religion, and theology	$ 25,788	20.0	4.8	11.7	31.5	32.0

Source: *Monthly Labor Review,* December 1995

computer/information sciences were among the five best-paid major fields of study. Among the poorly paying fields of study, for both sexes, were education, philosophy, and social work.

Earnings vary greatly *within* the major fields of study as well as *among* them. In each major field of study, some workers earn less than the median income reported for all fields. Thus the median for all fields of study for men was $43,199; but 18 percent of male engineers earned less than $39,001, and 9 percent of them earned $30,000 or less.[37] Furthermore, some workers in each major field of study had earnings that not only surpassed the median for all fields but also placed them among the top group of earners. Thus we find 20 percent of female philosophy, religion, and theology graduates earning more than $47,000—even though that field has the lowest median earnings of all the subjects covered in the study.

Not surprisingly, within most fields of study workers' earnings vary greatly, depending on occupation and years of experience. Thus, among male mathematics graduates aged 25-64, the median earnings of senior and mid-level managers approached $74,000; but those teaching elementary and secondary school had median earnings below $35,000.

No particular major ensures either high or low earnings. Still, graduates in some majors are much more likely to have high earnings, while those with other majors earn consistently less. The workplace, then, does not demand generic college graduates, but graduates with the intelligence and other personal qualities needed to master specific fields of study.

Simply getting a college degree, regardless of major, will not be all that helpful for those entering the twenty-first century workplace. The specific field of study matters a great deal—far more than simply getting a diploma. Students should therefore focus their energies on acquiring the specific skills and kinds of knowledge demanded by occupations that are both growing rapidly and paying well.

Jobs of the Future

Jobs and Employment in the Early Twenty-First Century

By 2005 the American economy will offer 144.7 million jobs, according to the Bureau of Labor Statistics "moderate" projection.[38]

TABLE 2-2
U.S. JOB GROWTH TO 2005
(Based on BLS projections. Numbers are in thousands.)

Total employment in 1994		127,014
Minus: Jobs vacated due to retirements and other departures from the labor force between 1994 and 2005	31,937	
Plus: Replacements to fill those vacated jobs between 1994 and 2005	29,491	
Plus: Jobs added due to economic growth between 1994 and 2005	20,140	
Equals: Total employment in 2005		144,708
Minus: Employment in 1994	127,014	
Equals: Net job growth between 1994 and 2005		17,694

Note that the total number of jobs to be newly filled between 1994 and 2005 consists of replacements (29,491 thousand) plus jobs added due to economic growth (20,140 thousand) for a total of 49,631 jobs. That is much larger than net job growth (17,694 thousand).

Source: Bureau of Labor Statistics N.B. 2005 is the last year for which the BLS has prepared projections.

That would be a net gain of 17.7 million jobs over the 1994 level—a 14 percent increase.

How is that net gain computed? It is the sum of (i) jobs added because of economic growth between 1994 and 2005, (ii) minus jobs vacated because of retirements and other departures, (iii) plus rehirings to fill vacated jobs. Table 2-2 shows this arithmetic.

How many job openings will be available to entrants into the workforce between 1994 and 2005? You might think that the answer is supplied by the figure for net job gain, which tells us how much total employment is projected to grow during this eleven-year period. If that were so, 17.7 million jobs would be available.

In fact, though, the figure is substantially greater. Net job gain yields too small a number, because it ignores the many jobs that will be refilled after jobholders retire or depart for other reasons. The actual number of job openings projected to become available to new job seekers consists of (i) the new jobs added by economic growth *plus* (ii) the hirings to refill positions that have been vacated. So the correct answer is almost three times as large: there will be 47.2 million jobs available to new job seekers between 1994 and 2005.

How will the mix of jobs in 2005 differ from 1994's mix? How will the 47.2 million new jobs compare to the 127 million jobs that existed in 1994? Which occupations will expand, and which will shrink? Bureau of Labor Statistics projections enable us to make some educated guesses.[39]

The Bureau of Labor Statistics has projected changes for the number of workers in more than 500 specific occupations between 1994 and 2005. As you would expect, different occupations are predicted to fare very differently: the number of personal and home-care aides is slated to increase by 119 percent, for example, whereas there will be 71 percent fewer letterpress operators. Table 2-3 summarizes the projections for nine major occupational categories.

Several interesting points emerge from the numbers presented here:

- Some occupations will obviously grow much more than others. White-collar jobs will grow rapidly: in particular, there will be a 29-percent gain in jobs for professionals and a 23-percent gain in service positions. On the other hand, the three blue-collar job categories (shown in the last three rows of the table) are either shrinking or growing very slowly. If we consider only net job growth, blue-collar jobs seem to be disappearing.
- But when we look at the more relevant number—job openings, as opposed to net new jobs—we see that blue-collar positions fare much better: the disparity between white-collar and blue-collar occupations is far smaller. It is true that positions for professionals, for service personnel, and in marketing will show the largest gains: in each case, job openings over the eleven-year period will equal 48 percent of all 1994 jobs. But there will also be many jobs to be filled in the three blue-collar occupations: openings from 1994 through 2005 will range from 26 to 33 percent of all 1994 jobs. Similarly, administrative-support positions—a relatively low-skilled white-collar category—

TABLE 2-3
PROJECTED CHANGES IN MAJOR OCCUPATIONAL CATEGORIES, 1994-2005

Occupation	Total Employment		Change 1994-2005				
			Net job growth		Total job openings (net growth plus replacements)		
	1994	2005 (projected)	Number	Percent change	Number	Percent change	
Total, all occupations	127,014	144,708	17,694	14%	49,631	39%	
Executive, administrative, and managerial occupations	12,903	15,071	2,168	17%	4,844	38%	
Professional specialty occupations	17,314	22,387	5,073	29%	8,376	48%	
Technicians and support occupations	4,439	5,316	877	20%	1,798	41%	
Marketing and sales occupations	13,990	16,502	2,512	18%	6,706	48%	
Administrative & clerical occupations	23,178	24,172	994	4%	6,991	30%	
Service occupations	20,239	24,832	4,593	23%	9,813	48%	
Agriculture, forestry, fishing, and related occupations	3,762	3,650	-112	-3%	988	26%	
Precision production, craft, and repair occupations	14,047	14,880	833	6%	4,489	32%	
Operators, fabricators, and laborers	17,142	17,898	756	4%	5,626	33%	

Source: Bureau of Labor Statistics

will grow by only 4 percent: but because of turnover, job openings in this field will equal 30 percent of all 1994 employment.
* Finally, the overall differences between 1994's job mix and the mix in 2005 will not be great. The similarity is well illustrated by Figure 2-2.

In short, technological change does not mean that blue-collar jobs and relatively low-skilled white-collar ones will disappear. In fact, about half of all jobs due to open up between 1994 and 2005 fit these descriptions.[40] In this respect the conventional wisdom—that such jobs are on the verge of extinction—is deeply misguided. Blue-collar and low-skilled jobs may be growing much more slowly than skilled white-collar positions, but they are not about to disappear. The nation's booming local markets, described in Chapter 1, are filled with producers of goods and services that cannot be imported. These producers will continue to employ millions of relatively low- and moderately skilled workers.

As noted, the conventional wisdom attaches too much importance to the fact that net growth in blue-collar and relatively unskilled white-collar jobs will be low: collectively, only 29 percent of net new jobs will be found in these occupational categories. But as we have seen, there is great disparity between net job growth and total job openings in these fields. The disparity results from the higher rates of retirement (and other departures from the labor force) that characterize these lines of work. Workers who have spent twenty or thirty years in physically demanding or uninteresting jobs are ready for early retirement, even on a modest pension. On the other hand, workers in technical or professional positions are far more likely to wish to continue working at least until the "normal" retirement age of 65.

Thus not that many professional white-collar workers are likely to quit their jobs or leave the workforce between now and 2005. But after 2010, when the first baby boomers will turn 65, large numbers of white-collar professional and managerial workers will seek to join their blue-collar and unskilled contemporaries in retirement. In the following years (for the period between 2010 and 2030), hirings to refill vacancies in the white-collar professions will actually surpass that category's net job growth.

Looking far ahead, we can say that eventually the share of blue-collar and unskilled jobs available to newcomers to the workforce will

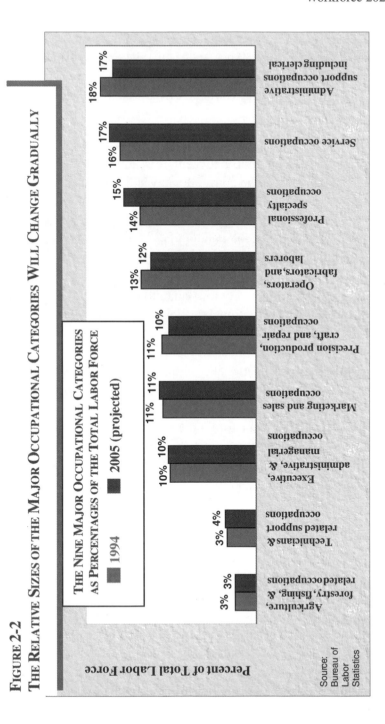

FIGURE 2-2
THE RELATIVE SIZES OF THE MAJOR OCCUPATIONAL CATEGORIES WILL CHANGE GRADUALLY

THE NINE MAJOR OCCUPATIONAL CATEGORIES
AS PERCENTAGES OF THE TOTAL LABOR FORCE

■ 1994   ■ 2005 (projected)

Administrative support occupations including clerical — 18% / 17%

Service occupations — 16% / 17%

Professional specialty occupations — 14% / 15%

Operators, fabricators, and laborers — 13% / 12%

Precision production, craft, and repair occupations — 11% / 10%

Marketing and sales occupations — 11% / 11%

Executive, administrative, & managerial occupations — 10% / 10%

Technicians & related support occupations — 3% / 4%

Agriculture, forestry, fishing, & related occupations — 3% / 3%

Percent of Total Labor Force

Source:
Bureau of
Labor
Statistics

shrink dramatically. Pessimists have anticipated this reduction for a decade or more. At long last it will occur—but about twenty-five years after it was first predicted to happen.[41]

Our task in years ahead is to improve our educational system and the functioning of our labor markets. We will need to do more to prepare new workers for an economy in which most jobs will require better skills and higher levels of knowledge than most entering workers possess today. What will the labor market demand in the first quarter of the twenty-first century? The best "leading indicator" is the set of particular occupations slated to expand most rapidly between now and 2005.

Job Growth is Most Rapid in the Best-Paying Occupations

Employment has grown rapidly in recent years: 9.4 million net new jobs were created between 1989 and 1996, and unemployment in the late 1990s remains at sustained lows.[42] What may be even more important (but is all too frequently denied) is that most of the new jobs are good ones. An authoritative study of job growth in the early 1990s found that 68 percent of new jobs paid above-median wages; more than half of these new jobs actually pay better than 70 percent of all American jobs.[43]

As our earlier analysis would predict, most new jobs produce services rather than goods. From 1989 to 1995, as the top half of Table 2-4 indicates, service industries accounted for nearly 83 percent of all net new jobs. Second in line was retail trade, which added 1,121,000 new jobs during the same period. Manufacturing, meanwhile, lost a net total of 1,332,000 jobs.

Do the new jobs in service industries involve flipping hamburgers at fast-food outlets? Are high-paying industrial jobs disappearing? That is the conventional wisdom, and if one were to look only at the top part of Table 2-4, it might seem consistent with the facts. After all, the service and retail industries, with average weekly earnings of only $371 and $225, respectively, pay more poorly than all other industries except agriculture. But knowing which *industries* are expanding or contracting their employment does not tell us which *specific jobs* are growing or shrinking. The

TABLE 2-4
EMPLOYMENT CHANGE FROM 1989-1995 AND
MEDIAN EARNINGS IN 1993; BY INDUSTRY AND OCCUPATION

(Numbers are in thousands)	Net job growth, 1989-1995		Median weekly
	Number	Percent	earnings,
MAJOR INDUSTRIAL SECTOR		of total	1993
Total, all major industrial sectors	6,679	100.0%	$ 394
Services	5,532	82.8%	$ 371
Retail trade	1,121	16.8%	$ 225
Transportation and public utilities	580	8.7%	$ 546
Public administration	388	5.8%	$ 555
Wholesale trade	357	5.3%	$ 446
Agriculture	207	3.1%	$ 252
Finance, insurance, and real estate	-22	-0.3%	$ 448
Construction	-65	-1.0%	$ 454
Mining	-88	-1.3%	$ 637
Manufacturing	-1,332	-19.9%	$ 452
OCCUPATION			
Total, all occupations	6,679	100.0%	$ 394
Professional specialty	2,599	38.9%	$ 617
Executive, administrative, and managerial	2,389	35.8%	$ 635
Service occupations	1,101	16.5%	$ 215
Sales occupations	975	14.6%	$ 314
Technicians and related support	240	3.6%	$ 495
Farming, forestry, and fishing	180	2.7%	$ 234
Administrative support, including clerical	-143	-2.1%	$ 349
Operators, fabricators, and laborers	-278	-4.2%	$ 328
Precision production, craft, and repair	-384	-5.7%	$ 490

Source: Bureau of Labor Statistics

important information about specific occupations is found in the bottom half of Table 2-4.

That part of the table tells us that good jobs are being created in abundance. Nearly 5 million net new jobs were created in professional and managerial occupations between 1989 and 1995; these positions accounted for nearly 75 percent of all net employment growth. As Table 2-4 also indicates, these are easily the best-paying jobs in America today. Meanwhile, only 16.5 percent of all net new jobs were in the service occupations, which (with median weekly earnings of just $215 per week) are indeed poorly paid.

The good news, then, is that recent *job growth in the American workplace has been overwhelmingly in the better-paying professional and managerial occupations, not in poorly paid service occupations.* That good news squarely contradicts the conventional wisdom, which is deeply mistaken on this point.

What is wrong with the conventional wisdom? It errs by focusing on industries rather than occupations. To judge the quality of America's new jobs, we must look at how many people are working in various *occupations*—not how many are employed in particular *industries.*

As Table 2-3 indicated, these prevailing trends are expected to persist into the next century. The high-paying "professional specialty" occupations are expected to grow by 29 percent between 1994 and 2005, faster than any other major occupational category. On the other hand, the low-paying "service occupations" are also slated to grow by 23 percent in these years.[44]

Growing and Shrinking Occupations

Table 2-3 showed how the major occupational categories are expected to grow between 1994 and 2005. Net job growth will be greatest in three categories: professionals, service workers, and technicians. These three categories will account for nearly 60 percent of all new jobs in these years. But what can be said about the more specific occupations that fit within these and the other eight broad occupational categories?

TABLE 2-5
THE 25 FASTEST GROWING OCCUPATIONS, 1994-2005
(As projected by the Bureau of Labor Statistics)

Occupation (Only occupations with at least 100,000 employees in 1994 are included.)	Employment		Net job growth (thous.)	Percent change in employ- ment
	1994	2005		
Personal & home care aides	179	391	212	118%
Home health aides	420	848	428	102%
Systems analysts	483	928	445	92%
Computer engineers	195	372	177	91%
All other computer scientists	149	283	134	90%
Physical therapists	102	183	81	79%
Residential counselors	165	290	125	76%
Human services workers	168	293	125	74%
Medical assistants	206	327	121	59%
Paralegals	110	175	65	59%
Teachers, special education	388	593	205	53%
Amusement and recreation attendants	267	406	139	52%
Corrections officers	310	468	158	51%
Guards	867	1,282	415	48%
All other health service workers	157	224	67	43%
Dental hygienists	127	180	53	42%
Dental assistants	190	269	79	42%
Adjustment clerks	373	521	148	40%
Sales workers in securities and financial services	246	335	89	36%
Bill and account collectors	250	342	92	37%
Emergency medical technicians	138	187	49	36%
Management analysts	231	312	81	35%
Bakers, bread and pastry	170	230	60	35%
Instructors and coaches, sports and physical training	283	381	98	35%
Food service and lodging managers	579	771	192	33%
All 25 occupations	6,753	10,591	3,838	57%

Source: Bureau of Labor Statistics

Table 2-5 lists the twenty-five occupations projected to grow most rapidly between 1994 and 2005.[45] Although hundreds of other occupations will grow as well, these twenty-five will account for an impressive 22 percent of the economy's net job growth during the period. Thus collectively they give a good sense of the sorts of occupations in which employment will grow between now and 2005. Significantly, eight of them—accounting for 55 percent of the new jobs to be filled in all twenty-five occupations—require great skill or substantial experience.[46] Nine of the listed occupations are in health care; most of the employment growth here, on the other hand, will be for low-skilled to semi-skilled workers.[47]

It is less than cheering to note that corrections officers and guards figure prominently among the sorts of workers predicted to be in highest demand. Positions in these two fields will account for nearly 15 percent of the new jobs in the occupations listed in Table 2-5. In other words, the crime problem is forecast to become still more worrisome in years to come.

Table 2-6 lists the twenty-five occupations projected to shrink most sharply during the same period (1994-2005). What conclusions can we draw by comparing it with Table 2-5? Two pieces of good news stand out. First, fewer than a million jobs will disappear in the twenty-five rapidly shrinking occupations, whereas close to four million will be created in the twenty-five rapidly growing ones. In addition, only 11 percent of 1994 jobs in the twenty-five shrinking occupations will disappear by 2005; but employment in the twenty-five growing occupations will rise by 57 percent over the 1994 levels.

What do the shrinking occupations have in common? In general, they require a medium level of skill or education: for the most part, these are actually not jobs for low-skilled workers. Most of the jobs will be lost because information technology (IT) is enabling machines to substitute for human labor. Computer operators, for example, are being replaced by better software and more integrated computer systems, which obviate the need for individual machine operators. Machine tool-cutting operators and tenders are being replaced by computer-controlled machine tools. Bank tellers are being replaced by ATMs and as a result of other IT-related changes in the banking industry. Contrary to what one might

TABLE 2-6
THE 25 FASTEST *SHRINKING* OCCUPATIONS, 1994-2005
(As projected by the Bureau of Labor Statistics)

Occupation (Only occupations with at least 100,000 employees in 1994 are included.)	Employment 1994	Employment 2005	Net job growth (thous.)	Percent change in employment
Computer operators	259	162	-97	-37%
Machine tool cutting operators	119	85	-34	-29%
Bank tellers	559	407	-152	-27%
Sewing machine operators, garment	531	391	-140	-26%
File clerks	278	236	-42	-15%
Electrical and electronic assemblers	212	182	-30	-14%
Machine-forming operators	171	151	-20	-12%
Electrical and electronic assemblers, precision	144	127	-17	-12%
Communication, transportation, and utilities operations managers	154	135	-19	-12%
Tool and die makers	142	127	-15	-11%
Service station attendants	167	148	-19	-11%
Mail clerks, except mail-machine operators and postal service	127	116	-11	-9%
Sewing machine operators	129	117	-12	-9%
Machine feeders and offbearers	262	242	-20	-8%
Bookkeeping & accounting clerks	2181	2003	-178	-8%
Payroll and timekeeping clerks	157	144	-13	-8%
Bartenders	373	347	-26	-7%
Industrial production managers	206	191	-15	-7%
Data entry keyers, except composing	395	370	-25	-6%
Insurance policy processing clerks	179	168	-11	-6%
Telephone and cable TV line installers and repairers	191	181	-10	-5%
Machinists	369	349	-20	-5%
Stenographers	105	102	-3	-3%
All other clerical workers	721	698	-23	-3%
Wholesale and retail buyers	180	178	-2	-1%
All 25 occupations		7,357	-954	-11%

Source: Bureau of Labor Statistics

expect, few jobs in these fields will be lost because of import competition from low-wage developing countries. (The loss of jobs for sewing-machine operators, though, may offer an exception to this rule.)

Now that we know more about the occupations likely to grow in years to come, we must consider the qualities that workers will need to fill the available jobs.

Skills for Growing Occupations: Will There Be a Deficit?

One of *Workforce 2000*'s important contributions was to identify an emerging shortage of skilled workers in the American economy. The book foresaw a gap between the qualifications of workers and the changing job mix of the American economy. *Workforce 2000* concluded that future workers would need to be much more skilled and better educated than in the past. It sounded an alarm, noting that in some respects the skills and education of the American workforce were actually on the decline.

Can a "skills gap" exist? In one sense, no: a free labor market tends to equilibriate the supply and demand of various kinds of labor. But in a second, perhaps more important sense, there can be a skills gap. *Workforce 2000* argued presciently that America's productivity (and hence its standard of living) would rise significantly only if its workforce came to be much better educated and much more highly skilled. *Workforce 2000* also stated that major public and private efforts would be needed to bring about those improvements. In other words, *Workforce 2000* raised a normative concern about a mismatch between the skills that might be available and those that would be most desirable; it did not predict imbalance in the labor market.[48]

Is the American economy changing so rapidly that the skills of today's workforce will be obsolete early in the twenty-first century? Must new entrants into the workforce acquire vocational skills that are much more sophisticated than those of today's jobholders? To answer these questions, we compare Bureau of Labor Statistics projections for future employment (by occupational category) with information contained in the Department of Labor's *Dictionary of Occupational Titles* (DOT), which describes skills needed to work in various occupations.[49]

The DOT divides cognitive skills into three "General Education Development" (GED) components: reasoning development, mathematical development, and language development. Each of these is categorized into six different levels, ranging from the most elementary (level 1) to the most sophisticated (level 6). Each detailed occupation is then rated according to the level required in each GED component.

In the following discussion we match Bureau of Labor Statistics employment projections for 422 specific occupations with DOT analyses of the requisite GED skill levels for these occupations. Overall, the growth occupations require much greater skill than the occupations in decline.

Whether we look at language, mathematics, or reasoning, Figures 2-3 through 2-5 tell essentially the same story: 99 percent of the jobs in decline require skills at level 3 or lower. By contrast, much job growth will be in occupations requiring skills rated at 4 or higher: for example, over 30 percent of expanding jobs will require reasoning skills at level 4 or

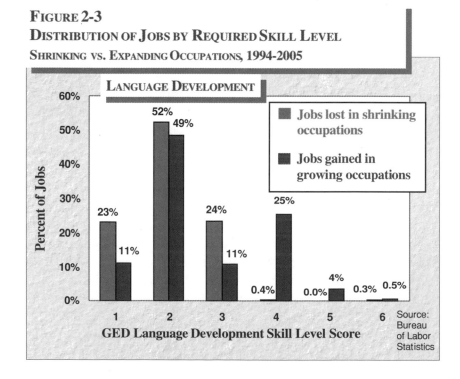

FIGURE 2-3
DISTRIBUTION OF JOBS BY REQUIRED SKILL LEVEL
SHRINKING VS. EXPANDING OCCUPATIONS, 1994-2005

LANGUAGE DEVELOPMENT

■ Jobs lost in shrinking occupations

■ Jobs gained in growing occupations

GED Language Development Skill Level Score

Source: Bureau of Labor Statistics

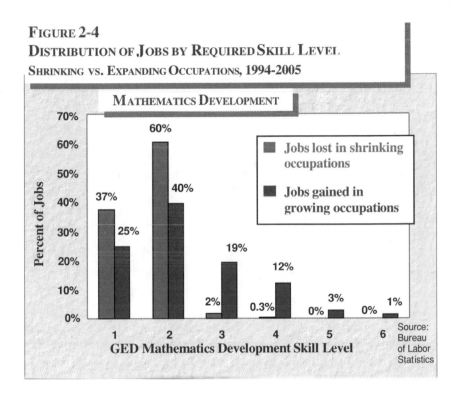

FIGURE 2-4
DISTRIBUTION OF JOBS BY REQUIRED SKILL LEVEL
SHRINKING VS. EXPANDING OCCUPATIONS, 1994-2005

above. In short, shrinking occupations overwhelmingly require modest skills, but high skills are called for by a significant component of the expanding occupations. The words of *Workforce 2000* still ring true: "The fastest-growing jobs require much higher math, language, and reasoning capabilities...,while slowly-growing jobs require less."[50] If anything, the case is stronger today than when those words were written in 1987.

Summary

Several conclusions emerge from this chapter:

- The American workplace is fast completing an evolution in which physical strength has become an increasingly irrelevant attribute,

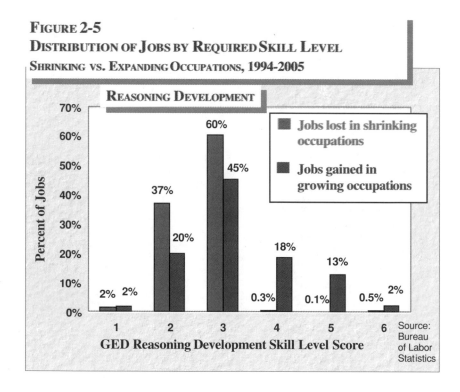

FIGURE 2-5
DISTRIBUTION OF JOBS BY REQUIRED SKILL LEVEL
SHRINKING VS. EXPANDING OCCUPATIONS, 1994-2005

REASONING DEVELOPMENT

Source: Bureau of Labor Statistics

while knowledge and facility with modern technology have become increasingly central ones.

- Demand has decreased for workers—chiefly male—who can primarily offer physical strength and endurance to employers, rather than skills and knowledge.
- More and more jobs can be done equally well by men and women.
- Although lifetime employment with a single firm is becoming increasingly uncommon, job security is not changing notably overall.
- Both temporary employment and work outside of traditional office settings (made possible by telecommuting) are becoming more common. Both of these developments generally accord with the desires of the workers affected by them.
- Although earnings have dispersed, and greater gaps divide the income of the well-paid and the poorly paid, income mobility

remains an important feature of the American economy. With sufficient ambition, ability, and education, individuals can still rise far and fast in this country.

- The average earnings of whites significantly exceed those of blacks and Hispanics. But blacks are increasing their earnings more rapidly than whites. Gains in Hispanic earnings, on the other hand, are lagging, because Hispanics are not improving their overall levels of educational attainment.

- The jobs that are growing most rapidly in number also generally pay the best. These jobs require increasingly high levels of skill and knowledge.

- The highest rewards go to workers with knowledge and skills that are relevant to the workplace. Generic college degrees in and of themselves are not in demand.

- Earnings vary widely both among and within major fields of study. Workers with degrees in some fields earn much more than those with degrees in others. Nevertheless, no degree guarantees either a high or low income.

- The American economy has created jobs with sufficient speed to absorb new workforce entrants. Unemployment is low in the late 1990s, and there is no reason it cannot remain low into the twenty-first century.

- The conventional wisdom attacking the quality of newly created jobs is wrong. On balance, the new jobs created in the American economy have improved in the last two decades and probably will continue to improve in the future. Increasingly, new jobs are filled by professionals and managers, who are very well paid.

- At the same time, the share of poorly paying jobs is also increasing, albeit more slowly. But proportionately fewer new jobs offer workers moderate incomes.

- Jobs that are disappearing require much lower levels of skill than jobs that are being created. Unless the education and skill levels of the American workforce are upgraded, America's productivity and prosperity will grow less quickly than is desirable.

CHAPTER THREE

THE WORKFORCE TO THE YEAR 2020

How will the composition of the workforce change between now and 2020? In this chapter we discuss three important alterations. A sizable cohort of workers will have aged, with some retiring but others staying on the job; the workforce is likely to grow only slowly; and its gender and ethnic mix will continue to shift gradually.

First, although the average age of the population and workforce will continue to increase until close to 2020, the workforce will no longer be "aging" very much thereafter. That is because many workers born during the baby boom will be leaving the workforce by then. By 2020, the oldest members of the cohort of 76 million baby boomers will be well into their seventies. Thus they will have begun to retire in significant numbers.

But aging workers may often be unable to afford retirement, because—as we explain later in this chapter—their sheer numbers will lead to sharp reductions in Social Security and Medicare benefits. Furthermore, many well-educated professional workers among the baby boomers will actually prefer to work through their sixties or even longer. The resulting continued presence of aging baby boomers in the workforce will face employers with two challenges: first, they will need to design benefit plans and workplace options that appeal to older workers wishing and needing to work past age 65; second, they will need to find slots into which younger workers can be promoted.

The exit of the boomers who do retire explains our second prediction: the workforce is likely to grow only slowly. For the most part, 2020's workers have already been born; even substantial changes in birth rates will not now have much effect on the size of the workforce. Still, two factors may significantly alter its size: the number of new immigrants and the rate at which individuals participate in the workforce. Because the baby boomers will gradually be replaced by a much smaller cohort of "baby busters" (those born 1965-1985), neither the workforce nor the population will grow rapidly. Still, national rates are composites, and some regions will grow quite quickly. Most workforce and population growth will occur in the West and South, while the Northeast and Midwest will grow far more slowly.

Because the workforce will grow only slowly overall, accelerated economic growth cannot be achieved simply by adding more workers, for they will be unavailable. Instead, workers' productivity must rise; but if it is to do so, we must improve our technology and our education. Unfortunately, the need to increase productivity will be particularly pressing, because the rate of workforce growth will be slowing just when more economic growth would be desirable: in its absence, many aging baby boomers will be unable to afford to retire.

Finally, the gender and ethnic composition of the labor force will continue to change, as predicted by *Workforce 2000*; but the change will continue to be incremental. By 2020, men and women will each comprise about half the total workforce. White non-Hispanics will still represent 68 percent of it (down from 76 percent today); 14 percent of the workforce will be Hispanic (up from the current 9 percent); and 6 percent will be Asian (up from today's 4 percent). The black share of the workforce will remain unchanged at about 11 percent. But here, too, these national aggregates mask great regional disparities. In particular, the Hispanic and Asian shares of the workforce—and total population—will grow much more rapidly in the West.

In this chapter we reach these conclusions by examining (a) the growth (and aging) of the total population; (b) the resultant growth (and aging) of the workforce; and (c) the gradual ethnic diversification of both population and workforce. We then examine the educational attainments of the ethnically diverse population of today's classrooms, as an indicator of the skills to be possessed by the ethnically diverse population of tomorrow's workforce.

Slow Population Growth Ahead

According to the Census Bureau's middle (and in its view most likely) projection, the U.S. population will reach 325 million by the year 2020, an increase of approximately 24 percent over 1995's figure of 262 million. But it is important to realize that alternative assumptions about fertility, mortality, and especially immigration yield very different estimates. As Figure 3-1 shows, the Census Bureau also offers a low projection for 2020 of 289 million Americans, as well as a high projection of 358 million. By 2050, the range widens from a low estimate of 283 million to a high estimate of 519 million, bracketing a middle projection of 394 million.

If the Census Bureau's middle projection holds true, the American population will have grown by a bit more than 1 percent per year in the 1990s. That rate is approximately 10 percent higher than it was in the 1980s, when the population grew more slowly than at any time since the Depression. The increase in the early 1990s was the product of an "echo effect": the baby boomers are now producing children themselves in great numbers. From the later 1990s until about 2020, the annual growth rate will again decline to the levels of the 1980s. After that, as the baby boomers pass into their seventies and beyond, the growth rate will plunge dramatically, to less than half its current level. But until 2010, the most notable change will be the slow graying of the population, as the baby boomers approach the retirement threshold.

How might the size of the population be affected by fertility, mortality, and immigration? Fertility may well hold steady in the early twenty-first century, remaining at its present rate of about 2.1 births per woman of child-bearing age; but it could also rise or drop slightly, as customs and economic conditions change. Mortality is projected to decrease, as life spans lengthen from an expected 76 years (for those born in the mid-1990s) to nearly 80 years (for those born in 2020). Mortality rates could drop even more sharply, though, if death rates from heart disease and

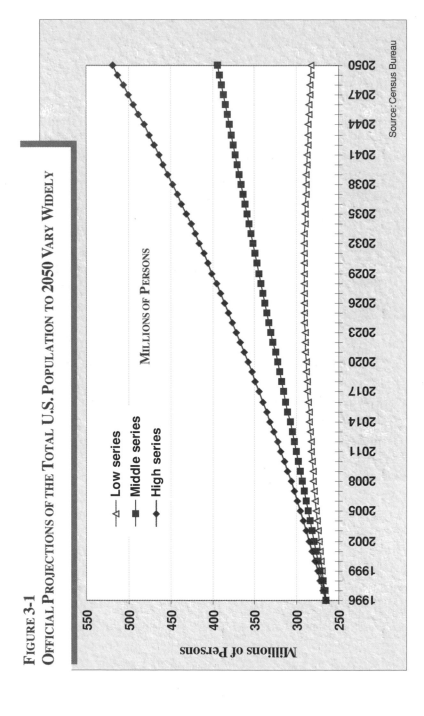

FIGURE 3-1
OFFICIAL PROJECTIONS OF THE TOTAL U.S. POPULATION TO 2050 VARY WIDELY

MILLIONS OF PERSONS

Low series
Middle series
High series

Millions of Persons

550
500
450
400
350
300
250

1996 1999 2002 2005 2008 2011 2014 2017 2020 2023 2026 2029 2032 2035 2038 2041 2044 2047 2050

Source: Census Bureau

stroke continue to decrease as rapidly as they did between 1980 and 1995. Conversely, increasing death rates from cancer and pulmonary disease could slow the trend toward longer life spans. Overall, though, changes in projected fertility and mortality rates are unlikely seriously to alter the population estimates for 2020.

Immigration is quite another matter, because its future levels are uncertain.[1] Currently, the Census Bureau projects that annual net immigration into the United States—that is, the figure that takes account of immigrant deaths and repatriations as well as arrivals—will remain indefinitely at 820,000. It is interesting to note that this level is roughly twice that forecast by the Census Bureau back in the mid-1980s. But even that figure may well be too low; the annual average for 1991-1995 was nearly 900,000, and the trend for the past several decades has been upward. Because tens of millions of foreigners would immigrate to the United States if they could, the actual number of future immigrants will depend entirely on what U.S. immigration policy is and whether it is effectively enforced.

Nativist and protectionist sentiments might well curtail future immigration significantly; on the other hand, a more liberal policy or ineffective enforcement could yield far greater numbers of immigrants than foreseen by the Census Bureau.

In any case, if immigration policy remains unaltered, immigration will be the chief cause of American population growth in decades ahead. According to one estimate, between 1990 and 2040 our current law could be expected to increase the American population by approximately 70 million—25 million immigrants and their 45 million children. That total would represent almost two-thirds of the net population growth expected to take place.[2]

Regional Disparities in America's Population Growth

The nation's composite population growth masks important differences among the various regions. Regional growth rates will differ remarkably during the next several decades. For example, approximately

82 percent of the nation's entire population growth between 1995 and 2025 will occur in the West and South, to which nearly 60 million people will be added during that period.[3] Meanwhile, the Midwest will grow only slowly, and the Northeast will barely hold its own. At the subregional level, as Figure 3-2 shows, the Mountain and Pacific areas are growing rapidly, as much as twice as fast as the national average. But the East North Central and the Middle Atlantic states show very little growth.

Just three states (California, Texas, and Florida) will account for more than 45 percent of the nation's total population growth between 1995 and 2025. California, which will gain 17.7 million residents, will show the largest population increase; Texas, which will gain nearly 8.5 million, will be next; followed by Florida, with a gain of 6.5 million.

The Graying of the American Population Will Radically Alter Social Security

Although the population will grow only slowly, average age will rise significantly. Figure 3-3 shows that the percentage of Americans under age 15 rose and then fell perceptibly between the mid-1940's and the mid-1970s. That change, of course, reflects the birth of the baby boomers, followed by their maturation. As decades passed, the boomers increased the proportion of Americans in other age groups. Between 1990 and 2010, average age will continue to rise as the boomers fill the cohort of those aged 45-64.

The aging of the baby boomers will profoundly affect the future of Social Security, beginning in 2011, when the oldest Americans born after World War II turn 65. In the decades following, large numbers of boomers will pass that threshold, all hoping to benefit from the Medicare and Social Security systems their tax payments supported during their working lives. In planning for their retirement, many boomers have counted on receiving hefty sums from these entitlements. And with good reason: as recently as the 1996 election campaign they have been assured that these programs would be protected.

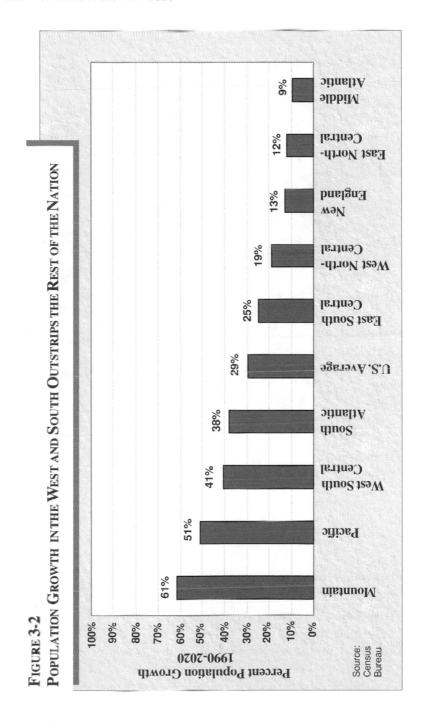

FIGURE 3-2
POPULATION GROWTH IN THE WEST AND SOUTH OUTSTRIPS THE REST OF THE NATION

Percent Population Growth 1990-2020

Source:
Census
Bureau

Mountain 61%
Pacific 51%
West South Central 41%
South Atlantic 38%
U.S. Average 29%
East South Central 25%
West North-Central 19%
New England 13%
East North-Central 12%
Middle Atlantic 9%

FIGURE 3-3
AMERICA AGES, 1900-2050 (projected)

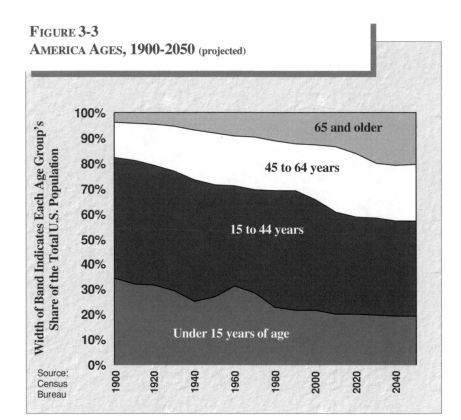

Width of Band Indicates Each Age Group's
Share of the Total U.S. Population

65 and older

45 to 64 years

15 to 44 years

Under 15 years of age

Source:
Census
Bureau

But in fact there is little chance that Medicare and Social Security will be nearly so generous by 2020 as they are today. The normal Social Security retirement age is already scheduled to increase to 67 by 2027. Brute demographic facts—the large number of aging baby boomers, considered in conjunction with the smaller number of baby busters financing Social Security and Medicare through payroll taxes—will almost certainly result in further hikes in the retirement age and less generous benefits. Boomers reaching what are now considered normal retirement ages may wish to exit the workforce, but many will probably lack the means to do so.

To see the problem, consider Table 3-1, which presents the ratio of people in their prime working years—ages 25-64—to those 65 and older. In addition, note that not everyone in the younger group will be

TABLE 3-1
THE RATIO OF THE PRIME
WORKING AGE POPULATION TO
THE ELDERLY IS FALLING

Year	Percent aged 25-64	Percent aged 65 and older	Ratio
1995	51.6	12.6	4.1
2000	52.1	12.7	4.1
2005	50.4	12.7	4.0
2010	52.5	13.3	3.9
2020	51.4	16.6	3.1
2030	47.4	20.2	2.3

Source: Census Bureau projections

working, whereas most of the older group will want to retire. The ratio hovers around four potential workers to one potential retiree until 2010, but then narrows to close to three-to-one by 2020. Furthermore, by 2030 it will decline to nearly two-to-one. This deterioration in the ratio of potential workers to potential retirees will not reverse itself for decades, even after 2030. It is therefore an unavoidable fact of life for most persons alive today.

The 1996 report of the trustees of the Social Security system projected that until 2011, the system would continue to produce a positive cash flow. As the baby boomers move into retirement, however, benefits paid out will exceed taxes paid in by an ever-increasing amount. Trust-fund assets will be exhausted by 2029 if no action is taken. A possible short-term solution would be immediately to raise the combined employer-employee Social Security payroll tax from its present 12.4 percent to 14.6 percent. By official estimates, doing so would close the Social Security funding gap with no cut in benefits for the next 75 years.[4]

But this proposal is unrealistic and ill-advised, for several reasons. First, it reflects the premise that the government will act soon to provide adequate funding for Social Security over the long term. But that will not happen. Changes in Social Security continue to be highly controversial—hence its reputation as the "third rail" of American politics. For that reason, alterations are not yet even on the table for discussion. And the longer discussion is postponed, the more drastic the tax increases that will be needed to maintain today's benefit levels.

Secondly, the officially projected Social Security shortfall derives from a 75-year projection based on demographic and economic assumptions that are highly uncertain. The recommended payroll-tax increase to 14.6 percent is a product of the Social Security Administration's "intermediate" projection, which assumes that productivity growth will be much higher and the Cost of Living Adjustment (COLA) to benefits much lower than they have been in recent years. In fact, even the "high cost" or pessimistic projection assumes that the economy will perform better than it generally has over the past twenty years. Therefore, the so-called pessimistic projection may be too optimistic as well. And even if it were correct, the pessimistic projection calls for a near-term tax-rate increase of 5.7 percentage points—a far greater tax hike than the 2.2-percentage-point increase mentioned earlier. It is highly unlikely that a tax increase of this magnitude could win approval.

Furthermore, to this point we have restricted our analysis to Social Security. But Medicare faces still greater near-term financial difficulties. The Medicare Trust Fund is scheduled to run out of funds in about May of 2001. "Fixing" Medicare without cutting its benefits would require an additional 2-percentage-point payroll tax hike. Yet to this point, discussions of Medicare reform have failed to address the hard choices of benefit cuts or tax increases, focusing instead on controlling the costs of providers' services as some sort of panacea. But imposing increasingly stringent controls is unrealistic, because providers are likely to curtail the services offered.

Current benefit levels in the two major entitlement programs for the elderly can be maintained only with the aid of steep tax hikes: taxes would have to rise by some 8 percentage points, and by twice as much if a solution is delayed. Given political realities, no such tax increase seems likely.

Nor, for that matter, would such a huge increase be desirable. Younger workers would object to handing over such a huge chunk of their incomes. An enormous tax increase would also cripple incentives to work: the result would be to court economic stagnation, high unemployment, and social instability.

In short, taxes will not and should not be raised drastically to maintain current benefit levels. Instead, by 2020 older Americans will face some combination of benefit cuts and later retirement ages. These developments will have profound implications for the workforce.

Slow Growth for the Workforce

According to the Bureau of Labor Statistics, the nation's labor force, which included 132.5 million members in 1995, will rise to 147 million by 2005. A "surprise free" Hudson projection puts the 2020 labor force at 171 million.[5] A second Hudson projection assumes—for reasons discussed later in this chapter—that many more older Americans will keep working. According to this projection, the 2020 workforce could grow to 182.5 million.

But whatever the size of the total workforce, it will grow much more rapidly in some regions than in others. The regional disparities in population growth we discussed earlier will produce similar disparities in workforce growth. Accordingly, between now and 2020 the workforce will grow far more rapidly in the West and South than in the Northeast and Midwest.

How can one estimate the size of 2020's workforce? In some respects, fairly easily. To begin with, almost all of its members have already been born. The Bureau of Labor Statistics restricts its count of the workforce to those aged 16 and above; and 2020's 16-year-olds will be born in 2004—a date that, temporally speaking, is just around the corner. Because all of 2020's 24-year-olds are already alive, fertility rates will have almost no bearing on the growth of America's workforce between now and 2020.

Similarly, barring unforeseeable wars, outbreaks of incurable fatal diseases, or medical breakthroughs, changing mortality rates are unlikely to alter the anticipated size of the working-age population by 2020. Of the three major demographic factors that, in the long run, determine the size and composition of the workforce, one might suppose that—as with population estimates—only net immigration could introduce substantial error in projecting them.[6]

As it happens, immigration has been and probably will continue to comprise a large proportion of workforce growth. Thus the foreign-born population accounted for 9.7 percent of the U.S. workforce in 1994, up from only 6.4 percent as recently as 1980.[7] New immigrants were responsible for about one-fourth of the increase in the workforce in the 1980s, but in the 1990s they account for fully half of it. The workforce currently grows by about 1.5 million a year; and each year approximately 500,000 legal immigrants, along with an estimated 250,000 illegal entrants, are added to it. As these figures suggest, the impact of immigration has changed significantly in the recent past; it could well do so again in the future.

But a second imponderable also exists, apart from immigration— the rate at which people participate in the workforce. If the past is any guide, that rate too can change notably over time. Thus the rates for specific population groups have been unstable in recent decades; for example, the participation of men has declined while that of women has increased. Figures 3-4 and 3-5 illustrate this point.

As we saw in Chapter 2, the percentage of American women who participate in the workforce has increased significantly over time: the figure now approaches 60 percent. Figure 3-4 shows that labor-force participation rates have been climbing since 1970 for all women except those aged 65 years and above. Furthermore, these trends seem likely to hold, except for young women aged 16-19.

On the other hand, male workforce participation rates have been declining. More than 85 percent of American men were employed in 1948, but that figure fell to slightly more than 70 percent in 1995. That decline is illustrated in Figure 3-5: between 1970 and 1995, labor-force participation rates dropped for men in every age category, but most precipitously for those 55 and older. Whereas 83 percent of men aged 55-64 were in the labor force in 1970, only 66 percent of such men worked in 1995. For men aged 64 and above, labor-force participation sank from 27 percent to 15 percent.

Many factors affect participation rates, but two sets of them are particularly noteworthy: education and skill levels; and Social Security, Medicare, and taxes.

FIGURE 3-4

FEMALE LABOR FORCE PARTICIPATION WILL CONTINUE TO RISE FOR NEARLY ALL AGE GROUPS

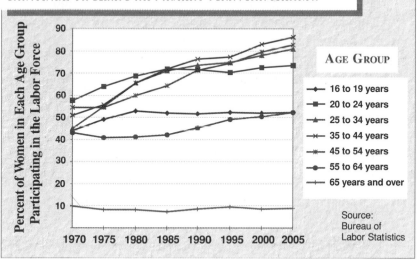

FIGURE 3-5

MALE LABOR FORCE PARTICIPATION FELL UNTIL THE MID-1990S, ESPECIALLY IN THE OLDER AGE GROUPS

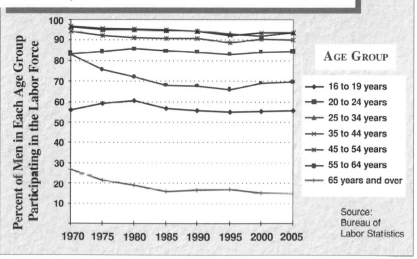

- After age 24, participation rates for men and women move upward sharply as education levels rise; better-educated people of all ages are more likely to work than those with less education. On the other hand, poorly educated and inexperienced workers who become unemployed are significantly less likely to find other jobs consistent with their education and training—at least in their own geographic areas.[8]
- Participation rates for men aged 65 and above have drifted downward for more than a century. More recently, generous Social Security benefits and pension plans—combined with high marginal tax rates on retirement income—have encouraged men to leave the labor force beginning at age 55.

How will labor-force participation rates change between now and 2020? Although no one can be certain, there are good reasons to think that they may be increasing in the years ahead for both men and women, especially for those in the older age groups. Participation rates for females aged 55 and older are certain to rise as a generation of better educated working women moves upward from the 45-to-54-year-old category. Indeed women's rates in the 55-to-64-year-old group have been rising steadily for more than a decade. And even the long slide in participation rates for men in the 55-to-64-year-old group seems to have bottomed out.

Rising average levels of education, less enticing retirement benefits, and a greater share of workers in professional occupations (where continued work is generally more attractive than in most blue-collar jobs) are likely to encourage men to remain longer in the workforce. In any case, the decision by more men and women to extend their working years could make a major difference in the size of the labor force and thereby help spur the nation's rate of economic growth.

Raising the Retirement Age: Implications for Labor-Force Participation

Delaying the normal retirement age is clearly a conceivable response to Social Security's looming insolvency. Its obvious consequence is that aging baby boomers would work longer. How would a trend away from earlier retirement affect the size of the workforce? Consider the projections based on radically increased labor-force participation rates for men and women aged 55-70.[9]

Figure 3-6 shows the implications of different assumptions about future labor-force participation. The "surprise free" line reflects the assumption that the trends projected by the Bureau of Labor Statistics through 2005 will continue to hold through 2020. The other line incorporates much higher participation rates for older men and women.

According to the surprise-free projection, America's workforce will increase at 1 percent per year between 1996 and 2005—a rate slightly lower than the actual annual increase of 1.1 percent for the period from 1982 to 1993. In other words, in this projection workforce growth is expected to slow—though it is still expected to grow more rapidly than the overall population, for which the Census Bureau projects 0.82-percent annual growth between 1996 and 2005.

The implications of slower workforce growth are potentially ominous. The surprise-free prediction of a slight decrease in the workforce's growth rate would mean slower economic growth, unless worker productivity improved sufficiently to compensate for it. In the absence of greater productivity, economic growth may be slowing just when it would most be needed, to enable the baby boomers to exit the workforce after 2010.

On the other hand, the alternative projection results in more robust annual labor-force growth of 1.3 percent from 1996 to 2020: that rate of increase could boost the nation's 2020 workforce by as many as 11.5 million workers—or nearly 7 percent—above the level that current trends would yield. Even if productivity does not accelerate, those millions of additional experienced workers could produce approximately half a trillion dollars of additional goods and services (in 1997 dollars) beyond what the national economy would otherwise produce. The taxes paid by these older employees—and the reduced Social Security benefits they would draw while remaining in the workforce—could contribute mightily to eliminating the fiscal disaster that looms if the Social Security system is not drastically overhauled.

FIGURE 3-6
THE LABOR FORCE WILL GROW SLOWLY
BARRING AN INCREASE IN LABOR FORCE PARTICIPATION RATES

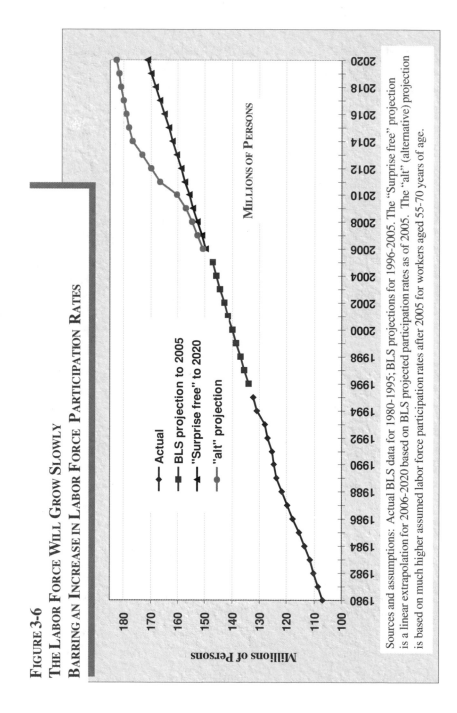

Sources and assumptions: Actual BLS data for 1980-1995; BLS projections for 1996-2005. The "Surprise free" projection is a linear extrapolation for 2006-2020 based on BLS projected participation rates as of 2005. The "alt" (alternative) projection is based on much higher assumed labor force participation rates after 2005 for workers aged 55-70 years of age.

More Older Americans Will Keep Working Longer

In fact, there is good reason to believe that the labor-force participation rates of older Americans will reverse their steady decline and begin to rise. Because real Social Security benefits must begin to fall, their decline can be expected to spur more older Americans to keep working. In addition, older Americans will be more likely to remain in the workforce insofar as they are better educated than their counterparts in the past. Better-educated older Americans—like better-educated Americans of all ages—are more likely to participate in the workforce. For example, as Table 3-2 indicates, the labor force participation rate for college graduates continues to average higher than 90 percent, fully 20 points higher than that for high school dropouts. Nearly 20 percent of men over 65 who are college graduates remain in the labor force, whereas less than 10 percent of those without a high school diploma do.

What explains this disparity? First, those with college educations are more likely to have professional, managerial, or technical jobs that do not require physical labor. In addition, such men have relatively higher incomes that are harder to replace; thus retirement is less attractive to them.

TABLE 3-2
LABOR FORCE PARTICIPATION RATES
FOR EDUCATED MEN REMAIN HIGH

Year	All men	Less than high school	High school grad	College 1-3 years	College 4 years or more
1970	93.5	89.3	96.3	95.8	96.1
1975	90.3	82.6	93.2	93.3	95.7
1980	89.1	78.8	91.9	92.1	95.3
1985	88.6	72.2	90.0	91.2	94.6
1990	88.8	75.1	89.9	91.5	94.5
1995	87.4	72.0	86.9	90.1	93.8

Source: Bureau of Labor Statistics

Older Americans in the Workforce: Implications for Everyone

The continued employment of more older Americans would be a welcome change. Their continued presence in the workforce would help ease the growing relative scarcity of "knowledge" and other skilled workers that will otherwise develop in the early twenty-first century. Thus the much publicized "downsizing" of the 1980s and early 1990s has obscured the fact that the challenge facing American companies in the late 1990s and beyond will be to cope with an increasingly short supply of skilled workers. The implication is that companies must now begin to consider how they can most advantageously tap this pool of older talent.

Furthermore, many older Americans will themselves be eager to keep working. To be sure, those whose working lifetimes have been spent in tedious and exhausting labor (whether of the blue- or white-collar variety) will probably want to exit the labor force into whatever retirement they can afford. Nevertheless, many graying boomers, their ranks reflecting the growing proportion of Americans in professional and managerial jobs, will prefer to remain active, employed, and earning. Indeed, many of them will justifiably believe that they are entering the most productive years of their lives. Furthermore, many if not most white-collar boomers will discover that their private savings and Social Security benefits fall far short of replacing their former earnings.

Thus both employers and other workers will have to welcome and integrate graying workers—especially professionals and managers—into early twenty-first century workplaces. But at the same time, the continued employment of more workers in their late sixties raises serious issues that need to be thought through and addressed. Americans are slowly becoming aware that the retirement of the baby boomers will pose financial challenges. But they have yet to realize that the boomers' prolonged employment will pose serious challenges as well.

First, as retirement ages become increasingly less predictable, workforce planning will become more uncertain. Human-resource professionals will find it hard to predict the date at which older workers will retire.

Second, the continued presence of top-level older employees may cause dissension among their middle-aged subordinates eager for promotion. Employers may need to create new "off line" or part-time positions for senior employees, to provide younger workers with opportunities for advancement.

Third, older workers will need different benefits. In response, health insurance might provide expanded coverage for the afflictions of the elderly, such as hearing loss and arthritis. Insurance providing for long-term care will be in demand. Because many workers past age 65 will have living parents in the over-85 "old-old" category, elder-care programs will become more prominent.

Fourth, health insurance itself will require massive changes. The current link between employment and health insurance is slowly fraying, as more jobs are found in small firms less likely to offer health insurance and as temporary employment grows. Indeed, as Figure 3-7 shows, the share of the population covered by employment-based insurance peaked in 1988; it has been declining rapidly since then. Employment-based insurance is itself an historical accident: it stemmed from attempts

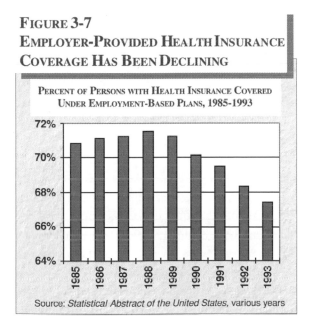

FIGURE 3-7
EMPLOYER-PROVIDED HEALTH INSURANCE
COVERAGE HAS BEEN DECLINING

PERCENT OF PERSONS WITH HEALTH INSURANCE COVERED
UNDER EMPLOYMENT-BASED PLANS, 1985-1993

Source: *Statistical Abstract of the United States*, various years

by employers to avoid World War II wage controls. (In response to employer demands, the War Labor Board ruled in 1943 that employer-purchased health insurance would not be considered taxable income for employees.)

As Medicare benefits decrease, boomers will be tempted to work longer, in part to keep employer-provided health insurance: planning ahead, though, they will also want their employers to offer health insurance to retirees. As a matter of fact, fewer employers now offer health insurance. In 1985, 73 percent of employees in medium-sized or large companies were eligible for health care after retirement. But in 1993, only 52 percent were eligible. In many cases the coverage offered was in the form of "Medigap" insurance, to pay for what Medicare would not cover. But as Medicare benefits decrease and its "gaps" (and costs) grow, employers will be still less inclined to subsidize their soon-to-be retired (and unproductive) employees.

These problems can be addressed only if American health insurance is fundamentally altered. Coverage today is skewed by tax incentives. Employees pay no income tax on the value of the insurance their employers provide, but if they purchase health insurance on their own, they do so with after-tax dollars. Both baby boomers and their soon-to-be former employers will have reason to want this system altered. Thus they might advocate repealing the tax exclusion for employment-based health insurance and replacing it with tax credits that everyone could use to help pay for health insurance. If tax credits were instituted, boomers wishing to retire would reap at least some benefit; and employers would enjoy the benefit of no longer being seen as the primary supplier of health insurance for retirees.

Taxing employer-offered health insurance as income would produce enough revenue to finance tax credits large enough to enable each taxpayer to buy a high-deductible health-insurance policy or to set up a Medical Savings Accounts. Younger voters might well support such a plan, if only to avoid the crushing tax increases that would otherwise be needed to finance entitlements for baby boomers. Once employment-offered health insurance became taxable, the link between employment and health insurance would disappear. By 2020, most employers will no longer provide health insurance directly to their employees.

Making Retirement More Affordable

Still, as the baby boomers continue to age, they will ultimately want to leave the workforce in droves: although there will be many exceptions to this rule, workers in their late sixties and early seventies are more likely overall to want to keep working (and to remain highly productive) than those in their late seventies and early eighties. Assuming a retrenchment in the benefits offered by Social Security and Medicare, how will these aged workers be able to afford retirement? We offer two observations.

First, the aging of the baby boomers makes welfare reform an even more urgent priority. More than four million households currently receive Aid to Families with Dependent Children. If the heads of only half these households found minimum-wage jobs, current payroll taxes would support more than 150,000 boomer retirees at current Social Security and Medicare benefit levels. Welfare reform is no panacea, but if transfer payments to the elderly face severe constraints, one option would be to lower transfer payments going to others.

Second, faster economic growth is essential. Continuing current 2.3-percent real growth would double the $7 trillion U.S. economy by 2028. But 3.5-percent growth would double it by 2018, which would provide vastly more revenue to the Social Security and Medicare trust funds. The rate of U.S. economic growth between now and 2020 will radically affect the severity of the needed changes in Social Security and Medicare.

Overall, groups that lobby on behalf of older Americans should shift their focus away from the ultimately unwinnable battle to preserve the levels of today's entitlements. A better strategy would be to advocate policies to help achieve the economic expansion that would minimize future reductions in Social Security and Medicare. To that end, such groups should support educational improvement, decrease in government regulation, and tax policies likely to spur economic growth.

The Gradual Diversification of the American Population and Workforce

White non-Hispanics have been declining as a share of the nation's total population for many years. In the 1980s alone, their share of the total population fell from 80 percent to 76 percent. That trend will accelerate in the twenty-first century; by 2020, according to Census Bureau projections, white non-Hispanics will comprise only 64.3 percent of the total population.[10]

The proportion of blacks in the American population has been rising gradually, and it will continue to do so in the future. By 2020, African-Americans are predicted to comprise about 12.9 percent of our total population, up from 11.5 percent in 1980.

In percentage terms, Asians are the most rapidly growing minority group in America.[11] Asians comprised only 1.6 percent of the American population in the 1980s, but the Census Bureau projects that the figure will rise to 6.5 percent by 2020.

In terms of absolute numbers, though, the most rapidly growing group is Hispanics. Hispanics comprised only 9 percent of the American population in 1990; but the Census Bureau projects that they will be responsible for more than 37 percent of our total population increase between 1990 and 2020. In 1990 there were more than eight white non-Hispanics for each Hispanic; but in the 1990-2020 period, considerably more Hispanics (28.7 million) will be added to the American population than white non-Hispanics (19.7 million).

Still, despite that rapid increase, a relatively small proportion of the overall U.S. population will be Hispanic in 2020—16 percent, versus 1990s 9 percent. As with demographic growth generally, however, the growth of the Hispanic population in the twenty-first century will vary greatly by region. By 2010, Hispanics (mainly of Mexican origin) will constitute nearly 26 percent of the population of the Western states.

The Hispanic population's growth will be extraordinarily impressive in California. By 2020, the Census Bureau projects, 42 percent of California's population will be of Hispanic origin. Asians will comprise another 18 percent, and white non-Hispanics will constitute only one-third of California's 2020 population.

To summarize, national averages suggest that America's ethnic and racial diversification is proceeding slowly if steadily. In 2020, white non-Hispanics will still comprise nearly two-thirds of the total population. But the national averages mask great regional differences. In particular, the West—the nation's most rapidly growing region—is rapidly becoming more diverse, as the Hispanic and Asian populations grow rapidly. In this respect California sets the pace for the region; it serves as a harbinger of how other Western states will change later in the twenty-first century.

It is obvious that immigration, recent and future, is the major force driving the process of Western ethnic diversification described here. We will become more or less diverse ethnically, depending on whether immigration policy is liberalized or made more restrictive. Note, though, that Census Bureau projections have traditionally understated net immigration. If current projections turn out to repeat that error, the Western states' populations will become still more diverse ethnically.

FIGURE 3-8
THE ETHNIC COMPOSITION OF THE AMERICAN
WORKFORCE IS GRADUALLY CHANGING

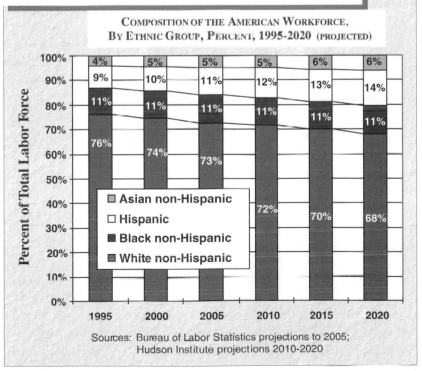

COMPOSITION OF THE AMERICAN WORKFORCE,
BY ETHNIC GROUP, PERCENT, 1995-2020 (PROJECTED)

Sources: Bureau of Labor Statistics projections to 2005;
Hudson Institute projections 2010-2020

Figure 3-8 shows that the ethnic composition of the nation's labor force—like that of its population—is changing only gradually overall. White non-Hispanics, who comprised 76 percent of the total labor force in 1995, will still account for 68 percent of it in 2020. The percentage of Hispanics will increase substantially, rising from 9 to 14 percent. The proportion of Asians will double, increasing from 3 percent to 6 percent.

Blacks will continue to make up approximately 11 percent of the workforce. As a result, the proportion of blacks in the "minority" work-force will shrink, falling from nearly one-half to barely one-third.

Although the ethnic mix of the national workforce as an aggregate is changing only slowly, the rate of change varies greatly from region to region. In the Northeast and Midwest, for example, workforce ethnicity is changing so slowly as to be barely noticeable. But in certain parts of the West and South, the changes are rapid and dramatic. The most dramatic case, California, is depicted in Figure 3-9.

Figure 3-9 shows the percentage of white non-Hispanics in each age cohort by year, from birth to age 85+. Thus in 1995, 57 percent of California males aged 40 were white non-Hispanics. But by 2010, that share will have dropped to 40 percent. The most precipitous decline in the white non-Hispanic share comes in the cohort of those aged 40-55. As these figures indicate, regional differences in the workforce's ethnic composition are already substantial and are becoming even more so.

The gender composition of the workforce is also gradually changing, but at a more uniform rate across the entire nation. In 1994 women comprised 46 percent of the nation's labor force. By 2020 the female share will have increased gradually to about 50 per cent.

Workforce 2000 and the Diversification of the Workforce

Our emphasis on the gradual pace of workforce diversification may seem to contradict the widely reported finding of *Workforce 2000* that the proportion of women and minorities in the workforce would rise dramatically. In fact, there is no contradiction: those who thought that *Workforce 2000* predicted rapid diversification simply misunderstood its message.

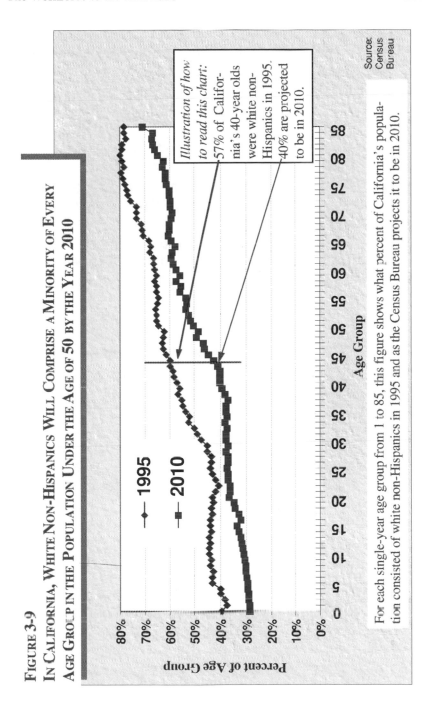

FIGURE 3-9

IN CALIFORNIA, WHITE NON-HISPANICS WILL COMPRISE A MINORITY OF EVERY AGE GROUP IN THE POPULATION UNDER THE AGE OF 50 BY THE YEAR 2010

Illustration of how to read this chart: 57% of California's 40-year olds were white non-Hispanics in 1995. 40% are projected to be in 2010.

Source: Census Bureau

For each single-year age group from 1 to 85, this figure shows what percent of California's population consisted of white non-Hispanics in 1995 and as the Census Bureau projects it to be in 2010.

With respect to the ethnic composition of the labor force, some ambiguous wording in *Workforce 2000* led to misinterpretation of the data. For example, the statement that "non-whites will make up 29 percent of the new entrants into the labor force between now and the year 2000"[12] was taken to mean that roughly three out of every ten new workers would be minorities. But *Workforce 2000* was actually referring to *net* new entrants into the workforce rather the *total* new entrants.

Table 3-3 should clarify the distinction made above. As rows 7 and 4 indicate, minority workers entering the workforce between 1994 and 2005 will comprise a higher percentage of the net new entrants (51 percent) than of the total new entrants (34 percent), because most white non-Hispanics who will be entering the workforce will simply be replacing the many white workers who will leave it. (See row 2.)

Although minorities will comprise slightly more than half the net new entrants into the workforce by 2005 (row 7), whites will still exceed minorities among total entrants by two-to-one (row 4), leading to only a modest decline in the white share of the workforce. (Rows 1 and 5 indicate a decline from 77 percent to 74 percent for white non-Hispanics.)

The changing gender diversity of the American workforce also emerges in clearer light from Table 3-3. Women comprised 46 percent of the workforce in 1994 (row 1). Only 41 percent of workers leaving the workforce by 2005 will be women (row 2). But 47 percent of workers who were in the workforce in 1994 and will still be there in 2005 will be women (row 3). Meanwhile, half of all entrants into the workforce until 2005 will be women (row 4). All of this means that 62 percent of the net new entrants into the workforce will be women (row 7).

This arithmetic can be confusing and lead to serious misunderstanding. *Workforce 2000*'s emphasis on net new entrants to the labor force rather than total entrants was often misinterpreted to mean that diversity training would be needed to accommodate the influx—whose size in any case was exaggerated—of women and minorities into the workforce. In fact, *Workforce 2000* emphasized more strongly that all new workforce entrants—including women and minorities—would need to be better skilled. We emphatically endorse and repeat this recommendation.

TABLE 3-3

HOW THE WORKFORCE COMPOSITION IS CHANGING: GETTING THE ARITHMETIC RIGHT

Row		Total workforce	White non-Hispanic, both sexes	All minorities, both sexes	Women, all ethnic groups
1	Total workforce in 1994	100%	77%	23%	46%
2	*Minus:* LEAVERS: Workers retiring and otherwise departing from the workforce between 1994 and 2005	100%	78%	22%	41%
3	*Equals:* STAYERS: Workers in the 1994 workforce who will also be in the 2005 workforce	100%	76%	24%	47%
4	*Plus:* TOTAL ENTRANTS: Those who will enter the workforce between 1994 and 2005	100%	66%	34%	50%
5	*Equals:* Total workforce in 2005	100%	74%	26%	48%
6	*Minus:* Total workforce in 1994	100%	77%	23%	46%
7	*Equals:* NET NEW ENTRANTS into the workforce between 1994 and 2005	100%	49%	51%	62%

Source: Bureau of Labor Statistics.

Workforce Skills and Education: Implications of Diversification

As we saw in Chapter 2, the need for skills among new workforce entrants—whether minority or white, male or female—becomes increasingly critical. We also took note of the fact that workers with increased amounts of education are rewarded, on average, with higher real incomes.[13] All workers, and particularly new ones whose working lifetimes will extend toward the mid-twenty-first century, will need to improve their education and skill levels.

Coupled with the gradual trend toward workforce diversification, these considerations should lead us to rethink our current immigration and education policies. Current law may permit the immigration of too many uneducated workers who will lack the skills to prosper in tomorrow's economy. And today's educational policies continue to generate significant educational disparities between white and minority students. On the hopeful side, there are signs that minority educational levels are rising, so that tomorrow's minority workers are more likely to be skilled. Still, it remains true that most minority workers will be significantly less well educated than most of their white counterparts in the year 2020.

With respect to immigration, on the one hand we saw in Chapter 1 that many highly educated immigrant workers play a vital role in our advanced-technology industries. Without their contribution, America's future economic dynamism might be put at serious risk.

But if some immigrants are extremely well educated, others are poorly educated. Thus 41 percent of the immigrants aged 25 or above who arrived here between 1980 and 1990 lacked a high school diploma; by contrast, only 23 percent of native-born Americans in that age group are not high school graduates.[14] Furthermore, less-educated Americans born here tend to be older, which means that they will not be participating in the workforce decades from now. Less-educated immigrants, on the other hand, tend to be younger; therefore, in years to come recent immigrants are likely to make up an increasing proportion of workers lacking basic educational skills.

In the future, therefore, we will need to raise the skill levels of immigrant workers—by providing training to those already on our shores, and perhaps by altering our immigration policies (to make education and skill levels more important criteria in deciding whom to admit).

The American educational system must also be improved if it is to produce more of the highly skilled workers who will be needed in tomorrow's economy. Without question, improvement is needed across the board—for the white majority and for ethnic minorities. No segment of the U.S. student population performs nearly so well as the best foreign students. Not only do U.S. students score below the world average in mathematics, but the top 10 percent of America's math students score only as well as the average student in Singapore, the global leader in math education. Our students are consistently outperformed in international math and science achievement tests by students in countries such as Singapore, South Korea, Japan, and Hong Kong.[15] In that respect, our educational system is failing to prepare a large percentage of the future workforce for the economic realities ahead.

But even though all American students need to learn more, it is minority students in particular whose futures are at greatest risk because they are inadequately educated. Thus educational improvement is particularly pressing for them. The disparities between white students and others may be decreasing, but only marginally, and tomorrow's minority workers can improve their position only if today's minority students are better educated.

During the past twenty years, white and Hispanic high school graduation rates have shown little movement, while black rates have increased by approximately 10 percentage points. The graduation rate for all whites remains nearly 10 percent above the rate for blacks and 20 percent above the Hispanic rate. If present trends continue, it will be more than sixty years before Hispanics reach white high school graduation rates.[16]

Scholastic Assessment Test (SAT) scores show a similar pattern. In 1990 Asians began to score higher than whites. Whites are also losing their edge to other minorities. In the past twenty years, blacks have increased their average SAT scores by 58 points, Mexican-Americans by 21 points, and Native Americans by 42 points. By contrast, white SAT scores crept up by only 2 points. Even so, present trends will have to continue for decades before minority students attain SAT equivalence with whites.[17]

Furthermore, the disparity between whites and minorities in college attendance is actually increasing. Twenty years ago, the white attendance rate was 3.9 percentage points higher than the rate for blacks and 1.8 percentage points *lower* than the rate for Hispanics. But by 1994 the white rate was 7.2 percentage points higher than the black rate and 9.5 percentage points above the Hispanic rate.

Other educational statistics also point to worrisome disparities. For example, whites and Asians are far more likely than blacks and Hispanics to complete a four-year undergraduate program in the allotted time. Only 43 percent of blacks and 49 percent of Hispanics complete their degrees on schedule, whereas 58 percent of whites and 66 percent of Asians do so.[18]

As we saw in Chapter 2, the workforce implication of a college degree is not the same in all disciplines. Here, at least at earlier stages of education, the trend is more favorable to minorities. Of the six broad undergraduate backgrounds (engineering, health, business, social sciences, education, and biology/life sciences), the first three yield the highest initial incomes. Education is by far the least remunerative concentration. Figure 3-10 shows that white students are more likely to be education majors than students in most minority groups. Furthermore, blacks and Hispanics are the most likely to be business majors, while fewer Asian and white students choose business concentrations. Meanwhile, Asian students are far more likely to be engineering majors than students in any other group.

On the graduate level, however, minorities tend to choose disciplines with less payoff in the workplace. Blacks and Hispanics who earn master's degrees are more likely to receive them in education, a low-paying discipline. Asians, by contrast, receive the highest share of master's degrees in business. Some 44 percent of all Asians' master's degrees are in business; the comparable figures for degrees received by whites, blacks and Hispanics, and Native Americans are 32 percent, 28 percent, and 25 percent, respectively. Asian students are also far more likely to earn master's degrees in engineering: 25 percent of all Asians' master's degrees are in that discipline, compared with 7 percent of the degrees earned by whites, 4 percent of those earned by blacks, 8 percent of those earned by Hispanics, and 6 percent of those earned by Native Americans.

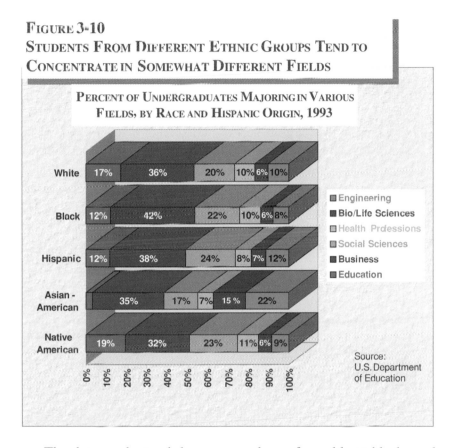

FIGURE 3-10
STUDENTS FROM DIFFERENT ETHNIC GROUPS TEND TO CONCENTRATE IN SOMEWHAT DIFFERENT FIELDS

PERCENT OF UNDERGRADUATES MAJORING IN VARIOUS FIELDS, BY RACE AND HISPANIC ORIGIN, 1993

Legend:
- Engineering
- Bio/Life Sciences
- Health Professions
- Social Sciences
- Business
- Education

Source: U.S. Department of Education

The data on doctoral degrees are also unfavorable to blacks and Hispanics. Blacks and Hispanics are most likely to receive doctorates in education, whereas Asians are most likely to obtain doctorates in engineering and the physical and life sciences.

Overall, the educational data offer cause for optimism about the future of Asians in our workforce. The trends for black and Hispanic students, on the other hand, are mixed.

All minority groups will make educational gains between now and 2020, both absolutely and relative to whites. Asians are already surpassing whites in educational attainment as well as in median earnings. But unless American education is fundamentally improved, blacks and Hispanics—two groups that are particularly poorly served by today's system—are unlikely to achieve educational parity with whites at any time in the next few decades. A renewed effort to improve education is clearly called for.

Summary

- The aging of the large cohort of baby boomers means that Social Security and Medicare benefits are almost certain to be reduced substantially by the time the boomers begin to turn 65.
- Slow population growth and the retirements of baby boomers ensure that the workforce will grow only slowly in years to come. Two factors will determine its growth rate: the extent of immigration and the labor-force participation of men and women (particularly older ones).
- As they age, some boomers will want to keep working, and some—particularly those involved in tedious and physically demanding work—will want to retire. But many if not most white-collar baby boomers will discover that their private savings and Social Security benefits fall short of replacing their former earnings. Thus they will want or perhaps need to keep working. Furthermore, many employers will need them to do so, because the labor force will have grown very slowly in the preceding decades. Public policies should change to encourage older people to stay in the workforce longer if they so choose, and corporations may need to offer new inducements to retain productive older workers.
- The nation's population and workforce will continue to become more ethnically diverse, but only gradually. White non-Hispanics will still account for 68 percent of the workforce in 2020. In Western states, though, and particularly in California, diversification will be more significant, as the Hispanic and Asian shares of the population and workforce rise rapidly.
- The gender diversification of the workplace will also proceed. Women will comprise half of the 2020 workforce.
- In the 1990s, immigration accounted for fully half of the increase in the labor force; if immigration policy remains unchanged, immigrants will constitute an increasing share of workers in the early

twenty-first century. Thus the job qualifications of immigrants will have an increasingly important impact on the skill and education levels of the workforce. Unless they acquire more schooling in the U.S. than they did in their native countries, recent immigrants will account for a rapidly rising share of the otherwise dwindling number of Americans who lack a high school education.

- Because economic growth will depend on increased worker productivity, the educational attainments of today's students raise an important concern for tomorrow's workforce. Educational levels need to be raised for all, and the continuing disparities between white and minority students are particularly worrisome. Overall, minority students are making greater educational gains than whites, but because their gains are only slightly greater, the gap in educational levels between white and minority students will remain substantial.

Chapter Four
Rising to the Challenges of Workforce 2020

This volume is not for sale at supermarket checkout counters, and we have made no effort to present tabloid-style predictions of an inevitable future. Our goal, stated at the outset, was to provide a road map—to describe the routes to the future that are open to American workers and the likely conditions they will encounter along the way. Here is what we have shown:

- The labor market of 2020 will demand highly educated workers who can create and apply sophisticated new technologies. Such workers will be rewarded handsomely. The labor market's demand for low-skilled workers will also remain significant but will vary from region to region. The supply of such labor is vast, however, because it is now available almost anywhere on the globe. Low-skill jobs that can be done by workers anywhere in the world will continue to disappear in the U.S. or be available only at depressed wages.
- Incessant waves of new technology and intense global competition and exchange will combine to create unprecedented volatility in the world of work. Firms and entire industries will rise and fall with surprising rapidity. Individuals will be buffeted by the waves, but many will learn to ride them to new heights.
- Dangerous, unpleasant, and monotonous workplaces will become much fewer in number, as the powerful trends favoring inventiveness

strengthen in America. Thanks to the computer and telecommunications revolutions, more and more people will choose to work at home, even if those homes are located to take advantage of scenery rather than nearby freeway on-ramps.

* The American labor force will become somewhat more brown and black in the next twenty years, but its most pervasive new tint will be gray. America's baby boomers share the hopeful prospect of living decades past the traditional retirement age. Many of them will want to keep working and will have much to offer.

Although we can speculate about how these roads and road conditions will intersect and influence one another in the future, we cannot offer firm predictions. The true nature of Workforce 2020 will depend on how many workers travel to 2020 via twenty-first century superhighways—and how many workers hit nineteenth- or twentieth-century dead ends. Individual savvy, corporate decisions, and the policies of federal, state, and local governments, in turn, will determine the choices that are open to individual workers as they contemplate the roads ahead. We all must understand that the time to shape Workforce 2020 is now. Before considering the policy challenges and before hearing our warnings and recommendations, consider the stakes. Consider two possible dispatches that might describe America in the year 2020.

2020: One America, Three Worlds

Today, in 2020, America consists of three worlds that function according to independent dynamics. In the first world, a relatively small elite of highly skilled workers—designers and manipulators of the most advanced ideas and technology—commands the highest earnings on the planet and enjoys lifestyles free of material self-denial. Whether they work in hyper-automated factories, in communal office settings, or in their dream homes, these workers are masters of their destinies, remaining in demand for their ingenuity and flexibility even when new waves of technology development engulf the planet or the economy turns downward in a particular industry or region. They are joined at similar levels of prosperity by the owners of businesses that fulfill the elite's unending demands for consumer goods, entertainment, and specialized services, often at the local level.

A second world coexists uneasily with the first. It is the world of low-skilled workers. At the upper end of a rather narrow spectrum, low-skilled workers whose jobs respond to local demand for services can earn a respectable living in some locales, though their prospects for advancement are limited. Many other low-skilled workers, however—particularly in manufacturing—are subject more than at any other time in history to the vagaries of economic cycles and to variations in wage levels on the other side of the planet. Families in this world are strained and often broken by lives on the economic precipice, further darkening the prospects of their children.

America's third world is made up of the permanently idle from the two other worlds. Some of its members emerged from the first world as they aged and pass their time sheltering or disposing of vast lifetime savings. Healthy and energetic but discouraged by tax policies and corporate indifference, they deny their still-considerable talents to the American economy. Other retirees, who depend heavily on Social Security, feel slighted by the decline in their benefits and are stymied by tax penalties incurred when they try to work for additional pay. Still other denizens of this world have more in common with those residing in the second world. Unskilled and often asocial, they no longer try to work, if they ever did, relying instead on an ever-dwindling pool of public assistance or on private charity. They look with equal disdain on the rich and on immigrants and other potential new competitors for their unearned subsistence incomes. Together with the second world's inhabitants, they constitute a social time bomb never far from detonation.

America's three worlds trade resources fitfully and suspiciously in labor-force and entitlement bargains meant to insulate more than integrate. Generational, jurisdictional, and ethnic conflicts plow deep furrows in American society and scar the nation's overall economic health. America's wealth is smaller and more concentrated than some say it might have been.

2020: The American Dream Never Worked This Well

Today, many see the American labor force positioned on a progressively more gilded ladder. At the bottom end, modest flows of new immigrants arrive in America to find a plentiful supply of low-skilled, low-wage work. Their numbers are kept in check by immigration restrictions and, more importantly, by the economic success of countries that once sent migrants and refugees to the U.S. Education firms the grip and extends the reach of immigrants and those ahead of them on the ladder. America's public schools are the envy of the world for their flexibility, accountability, and success in teaching, and large and small firms regard worker training as the key to employee satisfaction, productivity, and growth. Public assistance and private charity are generous but are geared as much to promoting work skills as to relieving poverty, which, perhaps not coincidentally, is uncommon.

The climb up America's workforce ladder is swift and rewarding. Two-earner families that work hard, stress education, and do not shun technology can enter America's large and fluid middle class within less than a generation and find unprecedented opportunities. The ranks of the middle class swell upward, not downward. An elite of the fabulously wealthy sits at the tapering upper rungs of the ladder; it consists of the extraordinarily talented or the incredibly hard-working. Their success breeds little envy, however, because the millions just below them never experience want. America's golden agers are encouraged to remain active workers and to share their experience. Their working hours and work locations seem infinitely flexible.

As a nation, America has never been stronger. Even the poorest Americans experience upward mobility within a generation. Correlations between race and economic success are disappearing. Social cohesion is strong, as all groups on the workforce ladder achieve ever-increasing prosperity together.

By design, the foregoing dispatches are caricatures. The first assumes a continuation of status-quo policies in the public sector and corporate world, while the second assumes genuine reform. Real outcomes can and almost certainly will be somewhere between the bleak and the utopian. Still, the dispatches describe genuine opportunities and risks. They highlight the qualities that will differentiate a robust and hopeful Workforce 2020 from a troubled one: a willingness to understand and embrace rather than to ward off the forces of change; the courage to expand the pool of workers in America through targeted immigration rather than merely to seal off our borders; support for work rather than idleness; and serious efforts to promote labor-force mobility rather than stagnation. Each of these qualities will be explored in more detail, after we briefly explain what is wrong with the most dangerous and counterproductive policies being peddled with the ostensible goal of assisting the American workforce.

What Not To Do

In our view, many familiar policy recommendations would move the country in exactly the wrong direction. Here, then, is a list of what *not* to do.

Don't Protect Sweatshops

Pat Buchanan, Ross Perot, and many others attempt to win political support by recommending tough import quotas or tariffs, particularly to protect low-wage industries (such as apparel- and broom-making), and particularly aimed at low-wage countries. Without protection, the sales pitch goes, industries will pack up and relocate to low-wage countries.

Putting aside, for the moment, the question of whether it is desirable for the U.S. to preserve low-skill jobs in low-wage industries, the underlying protectionist argument is empirically false. Industries have not left the U.S., Europe, and Japan in large numbers for Bangladesh, Somalia, Haiti, and Chad. In 1995, 72 percent of the stock of direct U.S. investment abroad was in industrialized countries, especially Britain, Canada, Germany, and Japan. Most of these countries, in turn, invest in the United States, not in developing nations. Less than a tenth of the manufactured imports of the major industrial countries derive from developing countries; the share of services imported from these countries is smaller still. Just 3.1 percent of the manufactured goods purchased in major industrial countries are made in developing nations.

Why is this so? Countries with very low wages have very poor productivity; hence the labor costs of the goods they produce can be quite high. Even in India and the Philippines, for example, unit labor costs are higher than in the U.S. But when productivity increases—as in South

Korea, for example—wage increases are rapid. Communication and transportation infrastructures in some countries remain poorly developed; and educational institutions in these countries currently show little promise of training workers to operate more sophisticated equipment in the future.

Ultimately, as we have argued, some low-wage manufacturing jobs will migrate abroad; many will also pay lower wages, closer to what is offered for comparable work in developing lands. However, the question for U.S. policymakers is whether SOS—"Save Our Sweatshops"—is an appropriate motto for the twenty-first century. Do the benefits of protecting low-wage jobs outweigh the costs of restricting free trade? We are certain that they do not. Artificially encouraging workers to remain in low-wage industries hinders labor mobility, shoring up yesterday's industrial losers at the expense of tomorrow's winners.

Statistical research has established that reducing trade barriers has a surprisingly powerful effect in increasing economic progress.[1] Open competition makes domestic producers efficient and raises real household incomes by lowering consumer prices. It also keeps businesses internationally competitive by decreasing their costs: protected steel makes cars and appliances more expensive; protected sugar and milk make for more-costly candy. In addition, free trade boosts productivity by rapidly disseminating information about what to produce and how best to produce and distribute it.

Finally, neither theory nor experience gives us any reason to expect that protecting low-wage firms from import competition will cause the resulting monopoly "rents" to trickle down to workers in the form of more or better-paying jobs. Instead, the benefits from protectionism are more likely to be used to purchase labor-saving machinery—or political influence via campaign contributions and payments to lobbyists. Industries that pay better, on the other hand, may bestow monopoly rents on their skilled workers; but the resulting payments tend to increase production costs and thereby make the protected firms less competitive than overseas competitors. In short, tariffs and import quotas increase the cost of production and the cost of living. Protected industries do not make the productivity improvements competition fosters. In the end, protectionism only impoverishes all of us.

Don't Demonize Technology

From 1811 to 1814, the English workers known as Luddites violently attacked machines and their owners, believing that machines destroyed jobs. Millions of machines and jobs later, books with titles like *The End of Work* or *The Jobless Economy* remain popular—even though similar books have proven hilariously wrong for two centuries. From 1900 to 1995, the U.S. population increased from 76 to 263 million, but employment increased much more significantly—from 20 to 125 million. We did not increase employment by destroying machines. Instead, we let machines do the worst jobs and kept the best ones for ourselves. The automobile destroyed jobs for blacksmiths and buggy-whip makers; the cotton gin destroyed jobs for cotton pickers; the automatic elevator destroyed jobs for elevator operators; and paper-towel dispensers destroyed jobs for washroom attendants. There is a name for this phenomenon—progress.

Physical capital and human capital often are complements, not substitutes. A software expert is useless without a computer, and vice versa. Whenever market economies (unlike socialist economies) have made large investments in physical capital, those investments have raised both the quantity and quality of job opportunities. But many such investments will be transferred to other countries if the U.S. labor force resists the technological challenge.

Don't Make it Too Expensive to Hire or to Fire

To read the coverage of corporate America in our mainstream press is often to believe that "downsizing" campaigns have consigned millions of loyal workers to near-poverty. Rare follow-up stories usually point out that most downsized workers find new jobs at or above their previous levels of pay, particularly if they are willing to learn a new skill or technology as part of the bargain. Nevertheless, the notion that firms must somehow be compelled to retain workers has a widespread following. It is, however, a cure that is worse than the disease, as western Europe demonstrates in a sad and ongoing case study.

Many European countries have high minimum wages, generous mandated benefits and leave policies, and strict regulations that make it difficult to dismiss any worker. The effects have been predictable. Employment has not grown and has often shrunk. France, Germany, Italy, and Spain did not create a single net new private-sector job in the entire 1980s, an ignominious feat in a decade of worldwide economic growth.[2] Unemployment in many European countries remains stuck in double digits long after recessions end and it would be much higher still if labor-force participation rates had not fallen sharply. Full-time employment must be accompanied by various mandated benefits; therefore, more work is contracted out or shifts to part-time workers (partly to avoid steeply graduated taxes). Because firms employing more than a certain number of workers are subject to costly mandates and regulations, firms tend to stay just small enough to avoid them. As a result, growth is discouraged.

Because it is difficult and expensive to lay off workers in most European countries, hiring is both rare and extremely selective. The obvious way to avoid being stuck with too many workers during a slump is to hire as few as possible in good times, even if it means (as it does) using too many machines inefficiently. And because employers are not allowed to find good workers by trial and error, credentials and job records carry exaggerated weight. Young people, who cannot have enough job experience to demonstrate reliability, have great difficulty landing jobs—despite the fact that European minimum wages are lower for the young. Youth unemployment rates in several western European countries are above 20 percent.

Better Ways Forward

There are much better ways to build a prosperous and dynamic Workforce 2020 than through the construction of walls to protect industries, firms, old technologies, or individual jobs. Our general recommendations can be grouped under four headings.

Understand the Challenges

First, we must be well informed about the challenges that lie ahead; to the extent possible, we must also embrace change. This recommendation is neither so self evident nor so easily accomplished as one might suppose. This report represents Hudson Institute's best effort to describe the general trends underlying the evolution of the American labor force. We believe that it is an essential starting point, but we do not imagine that it can take the place of detailed labor-force and economic-development analyses for specific regions and cities, industries or firms, and even individuals. Surprisingly little such analysis actually takes place, particularly in communities that seem insulated (temporarily) from economic downturns and in firms whose human-resource departments are stretched thin dealing with day-to-day demands.

In a detailed case study of a mid-size city in the Midwest, the authors of this report found ample evidence of the larger twenty-first century trends we have described here. (The leaders of the city in our case study asked that the city remain anonymous.) More importantly from the city's standpoint, however, we also identified several exacerbating or mitigating conditions specific to the city and region that warranted immediate attention. For example, a large majority of the workers at one manufacturing plant of the community's largest employer are eligible for retirement within the next ten years (thanks to an old and generous retirement formula). And recent employer-recruitment drives have seemed to attract more low-wage jobs to the city than might be optimal for its future economic growth. Hudson researchers tracked job and wage histories over time and helped the community develop plans for attracting and retaining high-level jobs. Armed with such information about their locales and firms, community leaders and corporate officials can formulate appropriate responses to the changes we describe in this book.

Expand the Pool of Workers

In marked contrast to the 1970s, when millions of baby boomers entered the job market each year, employers, employees, and government ments at all levels today must begin to adapt to a situation in which workers in general, and particularly young or highly skilled and motivated workers, are likely to be in short supply. Good workers willing to commute to traditional nine-to-five jobs will be even harder to keep, because there will be so many flextime and home-office options. This is all new, and it requires a very different approach to labor-force issues. Good workers are going to be valuable. They need to be courted, not discouraged. Perceptive state and local governments will bend over backwards to make workers feel that they are getting value for their tax dollars, and that it is worthwhile to work. Smart employers will be eager to attract and retain the best employees.

The political anxiety that there would not be enough jobs was understandable in the 1970s, as the baby boomers poured into the labor market. But the future will be quite different. During the 1992-96 recovery, the labor force grew by only about 1 percent per year.[3] As a result, the unemployment rate already is quite low in 1997. Without a big pool of unemployed workers to draw upon, employment cannot possibly keep growing by even the below-normal rate of 1.1 percent for long, if the number of job seekers is growing by only 1 percent per year.

Once the economy approaches the practical limits of full employment, there can be additional jobs only if more people are willing and able to work. If employment growth slows down to little more than 1 percent a year, to match the supply of new workers, the economy cannot grow much faster than 2 percent per year, unless productivity growth exceeds 1 percent per year. Yet the annual increase in output per hour among non-farm businesses averaged only 0.5 percent between 1993 and 1996.[4] In short, it appears that even if future economic growth is as low as 2.2 percent per year, employers often will have a hard time finding enough willing and able workers.

Meanwhile, even as conventional businesses still need workers willing to come to offices, stores, and factories for a specific number of hours, the share of self-employed or home-based workers in the overall labor force is increasing dramatically. The self-employed account for between 8.4 percent and 13 percent of the workforce, depending on whether we use estimates from the BLS or the Small Business Administration. From 1970 to 1995, the number of unincorporated, self-employed people rose from approximately seven million to 10.5 million—a 50-percent increase. Adding those who work part-time out of their homes, the number may approach 50 million.[5] The revolution in information technology guarantees that this trend will accelerate greatly in the future.

One school of thought contends that tight labor markets are not a problem, because they supposedly compel employers to give generous pay increases and make big investments to increase worker productivity. Unfortunately, limited supplies of qualified workers cannot so easily be increased by shifting income from business owners to employees. If increases in employers' compensation costs repeatedly exceed the increases in workers' productivity, as those untroubled by tight labor markets in effect recommend, then the cost of labor per unit of output will rise. If prices could be increased enough to cover those higher unit labor costs, the resulting inflation would ensure that the pay increases were illusory, not real. And if prices did *not* rise to cover the higher labor costs (perhaps because of foreign competition), then profit margins would be squeezed, investment curtailed, and workers laid off. Increasing inflation and lowering profit margins are unlikely to encourage more productivity-enhancing business investment.

The better hope for dealing with America's growing labor shortage is selective immigration. In "The Myth of the Coming Labor Shortage," Lawrence Mishel and Ruy A. Teixeira argue that immigration can and will be increased by a huge amount every year, to raise labor-force growth by 15-40 percent (e.g., from 1 percent to 1.15-1.4 percent).[6] But even if we were to admit substantially more immigrants, annual increases in the supply of relatively skilled workers would remain low unless the priorities of immigration policy were revised dramatically. By 1988, the foreign-born already accounted for more than one fifth of all U.S. residents without a high school degree. That fraction is rising rapidly.[7] Unless immigration criteria are changed to emphasize schooling and skills rather than family reunification and the need to provide a haven for refugees, a huge increase in the already large numbers of unskilled and unschooled immigrants might provide the economy with more workers but not more *qualified* workers. Criteria for admitting immigrants should therefore be altered to ensure that more new entrants have sufficient human or financial capital to become productive workers or entrepreneurs.

Increase Workforce Participation

Other than increasing the available pool of skilled workers through immigration, the most obvious route to alleviating an impending labor shortage is to increase labor-force participation among the existing adult population—the percentage of working-age people who are either working or looking for work. If government and corporate policymakers make work attractive, participation rates can increase in the U.S., particularly if older workers are kept on.

In earlier chapters we have argued that the past trend toward premature retirement is likely to be reversed in the near future, as a more educated group reaches the ages of 50 to 64. Well-educated workers typically delay retirement, presumably because their work is more enjoyable than menial labor, pays a higher salary, or both. Between now and the year 2010, the feared "graying of America" does not necessarily mean that huge numbers of retirees will be dependent on young taxpayers. Instead, it can mean that a larger share of the workforce will consist of experienced and dependable workers. (Some of these older workers may be unfamiliar with information technology, but that technology is also becoming more user-friendly.) The percentage of Americans over age 65 is expected to rise from 12.5 percent in 1992 to 16.5 percent in 2020—and far more sharply thereafter as the baby boomers continue to age. What we may see, however, is an older workforce rather than many more retired people—if policies do not discourage older people from working, as Social Security currently does. Older workers lose half their benefits now if they earn more than a trivial sum, and they pay income tax on 50-85 percent of any remaining benefits. The payroll tax also penalizes working spouses, who receive few or no additional benefits in return for the additional taxes they pay.

In the future, for firms as well as governments, encouraging workforce participation also will mean accommodating unconventional working arrangements. The companionship and learning that come from working with others, face to face, bring undeniable benefits. On balance, though, millions of people (particularly the elderly and women with children) are going to find it increasingly easy and attractive to do most or all of their work at home. Far-sighted localities will encourage this trend, by not imposing onerous zoning restrictions or taxes on home-based enterprises that do not make residential areas less attractive in any way.

For their part, employers will need to be creative in recruiting and retaining workers. The most skilled, innovative, and industrious workers will have the most options: they can start their own firms or consult. To attract and retain such talented workers for their firms, employers will need to accommodate their desires. Older workers are likely to want to be able to work at home a few days each month. Women with young children will be attracted by "family friendly" policies such as flexible scheduling, job sharing, and on-site or subsidized day care. Companies that provide such flexibility or family-friendly benefits will, in many cases, be able to attract and retain qualified workers without paying as much in salary and traditional benefits as other companies that do not cater to such specific needs. Jobs of the future will lend themselves to these arrangements to a greater extent than in the past.

Promote Upward Mobility Through Job Training and Education

Upward mobility through the labor force depends on education and skill levels. American education must therefore be upgraded at every level if America is to produce enough workers to make use of the available opportunities.

At the federal level, there are approximately 150 education and training programs which cost around $25 billion a year. Federal job-training programs are notoriously ineffective, however—or at least extremely expensive, when their meager results are considered. They are highly regulated by the federal government and were created for a different era and economy. Training people for the workforce and matching potential workers and potential employees is an inherently decentralized, local enterprise. Individuals who are armed with timely information about employment opportunities figure out for themselves which skills are most likely to advance their careers. The problem today is that most people do not have access to good information about labor markets or quality education programs that suit their interests and abilities. Labor market information programs operated by state governments funded through employer taxes are not designed to provide this type of consumer information. In most communities, no one entity is responsible for or assumes the role of providing labor market or career development information to adults preparing for or already in the workforce (not to mention the inadequacy of high school and college career counseling for young people making career decisions).

States and cities have already begun experimenting with promising new techniques of putting people to work, in which they learn by doing. Some of the most effective programs have involved subcontracting the task to private placement firms such as America Works and Manpower, Inc.[8] For the federal government to devolve this responsibility without freeing up revenues, however, would be unreasonable. Most of the 150 federal training programs should be eliminated, and federal taxes should be reduced accordingly, particularly where they have drawn from traditional sources of state revenue (such as excise taxes).

On the private side, a 1995 study by *Training, Inc.* magazine found that 43 percent of firms surveyed offered remedial education, defined in its broadest sense, including training in a host of academic skills.[9] The magazine found that 22 percent of employers offered training in basic skills such as reading, writing, arithmetic, and English. That is an astounding figure because 67 percent of those receiving remedial education are high school graduates. On-the-job training, whether formal or not, is extremely important. But why should companies be expected to remedy the deficiencies of our schools?

Primary Education Comes First

Early education is the most cost-effective way to decrease the number of unskilled adults in the future. Adult education often involves a prohibitively high "opportunity cost" for low-income workers, because time spent in school could be spent earning an income. Adult education also tends to be stigmatized: a "generalized equivalency diploma" (GED) is not thought to be as good as an ordinary high school diploma. If America could increase the number of traditional high school graduates with appropriate reading, writing, mathematics, reasoning, and computer skills, it could go a long way toward filling available jobs and laying a suitable foundation on which workers could upgrade their skills once in the workforce.

Despite the importance of primary and secondary education, however, and despite more than a decade of education reform since the publication of *A Nation at Risk* in 1983 and *Workforce 2000* in 1987, American schools have not made widespread improvements in preparing entry-level workers. In recent surveys, only 28 percent of fourth graders were proficient or better at what is commonly regarded as a fourth-grade reading level, and only 21 percent of eighth graders were proficient or better at eighth-grade math. Particularly troubling is that despite some gains in the past ten years, there is still a wide gap between whites and nonwhites on such measures as achievement-test scores and graduation rates. At present rates of progress, it will take decades to close these gaps completely.

The charge to teachers, parents, and students is clear—work harder, expect more, and focus on the basics. Schools need to set high academic standards for all children, regardless of their family backgrounds. Those supervising public education must set high standards, rewarding students, teachers, parents, principals, superintendents, and school boards that meet and exceed those standards—and penalizing those that fail to meet them. Communities need to specify in detail the minimum knowledge and skill levels children must achieve in each grade, and to provide for accountability to ensure that the common standards are enforced. No one should be able to leave high school with a diploma without having to demonstrate a high level of achievement in reading, writing, math, reasoning, and computing. Few states and communities in the U.S. can currently claim such assurances.

In addition to establishing academic standards, America must consider new approaches to public education. The one-size-fits-all structure in place today has not changed appreciably since the late 1800s, even as tremendous changes have occurred in other institutions. The 1990s are thought to be the era of "reinventing government": we are reconsidering which services government should provide, and changing the ways in which many government services—from garbage collection to prison and airport management—are provided. Yet public education has been largely impervious to this transformation, if not openly hostile to it. America still defines public education as an institution exclusively financed and operated by the government. Indeed, public education remains the last of the major monopolies. More than a decade of failed education reform, during which spending on schools almost tripled, convinces us that the system is incapable of renewing itself and is unlikely to do so without competitive pressure.

Several approaches to injecting competition are being tried on a small scale in various places. Most notably, charter schools have been created. New forms of public school run by teachers, parents, community organizations, and private companies, charter schools adopt various approaches to education. Parents elect to enroll their children in these schools insofar as the schools seem likely to meet their children's needs. Charter schools cost no more than regular public schools (and often less), and they are far less bureaucratized and burdened by regulations. They are held accountable for their performance by the public body that chartered them—in most cases a local or state school board. Early evaluations by researchers at Hudson Institute suggest that charter schools can improve the basic education of America's youth while placing healthy competitive pressure on regular public schools.[10]

Other attempts at injecting competition into primary and secondary education have not spread so far. Some cities have tried voucher programs, in which the tax dollars appropriated for education go directly to low-income parents instead of to schools. Using these vouchers, parents are able to choose the schools that best fit their children's needs, whether public or private. This is a luxury upper-income families already enjoy, but it is not ordinarily available to low-income parents, many of whom live in large cities with terrible public schools. Several privately funded voucher programs now exist in urban areas, as well as two publicly funded programs. Preliminary evidence suggests that participation in these programs increases achievement by students in them, particularly when compared to their peers unable to take advantage of the vouchers.

Don't Lower Higher Education

Americans are infatuated with the college degree, and it is understandable why. College degrees have served as the ticket to the middle class and, in the past decade, have paid off handsomely. As we point out in Chapter 2, college degree holders generally were the only ones to experience real gains in earnings during the past ten years. It may be time for Americans to adopt a more nuanced approached, however, recognizing that bachelor's degrees sometimes are neither necessary nor sufficient for success in the marketplace.

In the early twenty-first century, the best-paying jobs will demand high skill levels, particularly in the areas of reading, writing, math, reasoning, and computing. A larger share of fast-growing occupations also will require education beyond high school, but not necessarily a four-year college degree. Yet a recent annual survey showed that more students than ever are applying to four-year colleges, even though many of these students are poorly prepared. In most medium-sized to large colleges, at least one-fourth of the freshmen require remedial education in mathematics and reading before they can do college-level work. Even remediation is often insufficient. According to the U.S. Department of Education's most recent comprehensive study of adult literacy, 14-16 percent of American-born college graduates are functionally illiterate in math and reading.

The more nuanced role of higher education in the development of the workforce became clear in the *Workforce 2020* team's case study, mentioned earlier.

As in other places around the country, in our case study city the percentage of high school graduates attending post-secondary education has increased steadily over the years and now approaches 60 percent. The number of adults attending college either full- or part-time also has grown steadily. The community has two post-secondary institutions; one is a branch of a large state-supported university, and the other is a state-supported vocational-technical institution. In recent years, the branch of the university has become the number one choice of the community's high school graduates. About one-fourth of all the students entering that institution take remediation courses in reading and/or math. More than half of all bachelor's degrees from the university are granted in "general studies"; the only other two undergraduate degrees offered are in psychology and elementary education. Students graduating from this institution with these degrees find it difficult to find well-paying jobs in the community, which is heavily manufacturing-based. Indeed, many of the graduates from the local college work in the local outlet mall as managers and assistant managers of stores. Meanwhile, employers complain about a shortage of technically trained employees and seek to fill technical and professional jobs, many paying twice the salary of the store managers, from outside the community. When the director of the branch university was asked about this apparent mismatch between degrees offered at the university and employer needs, his response was that a "college degree is a college degree and it doesn't really matter what someone gets a degree in." He is wrong.

Our experience with the vocational-technical college in that community also highlights some of the problems with this type of institution in meeting the needs of workers and employers. Although the institution attempts to meet the needs of local employers, its funding comes from the state legislature, and the school's officials lack the flexibility to react quickly to the training needs of local employers. The school also lacks a working relationship with the branch university; credits do not transfer between the two institutions.

Our case study raised a number of important issues regarding higher education's role in workforce development which are applicable more generally in the U.S.

Lack of consumer information. Parents and students of all ages lack good information about the job market and appropriate education programs to succeed in the market. It is not true that just any type of true college degree assures financial success or a rewarding career. Further, there are differences in quality among programs, and people often do not have good information on how to distinguish among them.

Quality. Anecdotal evidence from professors and employers suggests that higher education has lowered its standards and the rigor of its curriculum to accommodate the large numbers of people enrolling. It is a common refrain from employers that a college degree does not mean what it used to. If this is true, employers are not only getting less qualified workers when they hire college graduates, but graduates may be getting a false sense of their own qualifications and may be surprised to find themselves unqualified to fill available high-skill jobs in the future.

Proposals to make the first two years of college "universal" for all Americans may have the unintended consequences of further lowering the rigor of the curriculum and sidetracking many young people into degree programs for which they are not suited. Colleges and universities should not become substitutes for a quality high school education.

Mismatch between higher education and the economy. Our analysis indicates a mismatch between higher education and economic conditions and trends. In a study Hudson Institute conducted on higher education in 1996, we found that more degrees in the United States are awarded in home economics than in mathematics, and more in "protective services" than in all the physical sciences combined. Yet as we have seen in earlier chapters of this book, the growth categories of jobs are in technical, professional, and managerial fields. Colleges are largely inflexible in responding to labor market demands because of funding mechanisms and tenure systems. This lack of responsiveness to market conditions could account for the growth in enrollment in proprietary post-secondary schools such as ITT and DeVry. While we do not believe that institutions should offer only degrees that lead to well-paying jobs, we do question whether all degree programs (in public-sector institutions particularly) should be subsidized to the same extent by tax dollars, when there are profound mismatches between employer needs and available education programs.

These views could be interpreted by some as opposing liberal arts education. That is not at all our intention. A quality liberal arts education provides a strong foundation of knowledge, communication, and analytical skills needed for life-long learning. Nonetheless, not everyone is suited to a liberal arts education and can make the connection between that type of education and the labor market. The challenge for today's colleges and universities is to create an array of options for people to use in continuously upgrading their education and skills. A growing proprietary sector and programs and degrees from a small group of colleges offered through the Internet show promise of expanding education options. These and other innovations should be encouraged. Although the pace of change is slow, the landscape of higher education will and should look much different in 2020 than it does today.

Rising to the Challenges

The journey to Workforce 2020 is a journey to an uncertain destination. In twenty years, observers may conclude that the American dream has never worked better, increasing the prosperity of millions of people and using the talents of the nation in a manner that promotes general well-being. But the road map laid out here could lead to another, more disturbing destination—an America that divides more than ever into a society of haves and have-nots based on access to the best jobs. Though our destination is uncertain from the vantage point of the late 1990s, we believe that there is much that policymakers, corporate officials, and individual Americans can do to steer the nation in the right direction.

The challenges are not simple, however, and we reject the unsophisticated responses that have become so prevalent of late. The recommendations outlined in this chapter are not intended to be definitive or exhaustive but merely to illustrate the most promising directions of change. Hudson Institute's *Workforce 2020* team looks forward to developing its own ideas further and to examining the specific concerns and proposals of governments, firms, and others. Our approach, which we recommend to others, is to adhere to three principles:

- Governments, firms, and individuals must base decisions and reform on the best information. We live in a time of information overload and yet often rely on anecdotes and outdated conventional wisdom in making important decisions. Corporate and government leaders must understand the full dimensions of the labor-force challenges they confront.
- America must adapt the institutions shaping its labor force to new circumstances. We cannot produce twenty-first century knowledge workers in nineteenth century public schools, early-twentieth century higher education institutions, or mid-twentieth century federal job-training programs.
- Society-wide solutions will not address America's workforce challenges adequately. Instead, the challenges ahead call for solutions tailored to individual circumstances. One size does not fit all individuals, all firms, all regions, or all levels of government. Individual

and local experimentation must be the order of the day, to promote competition in some instances and increased knowledge in others.

The twenty-first century holds incredible promise for America's workers. Workforce 2020 can be the most prosperous, flexible, intellectually stimulated, and safest workforce the world has ever known. But we can achieve this goal only if we take personal responsibility as individuals, parents, employers, and citizens. We need to understand our situation and confront our challenges. Outmoded government programs, corporate practices, and individual traits must be altered if we are to cope successfully with the new economic realities that are fast approaching. Our actions today will determine whether we realize our hope for a competent and prosperous workforce tomorrow.

NOTES

CHAPTER ONE

[1] Joseph A. Schumpeter, *Capitalism, Socialism, and Democracy*, 3rd ed., Harper & Brothers, New York, pp. 81-86.

[2] Sources for the section on the semiconductor industry are *McGraw Hill Encyclopedia of Science and Technology;* Les Freed, *The History of Computers,* Ziff-Davis Press, 1995; and Francisco A. Moris, "Semiconductors: the building blocks of the information revolution," *Monthly Labor Review*, August 1996, pp. 6-17.

[3] Sources for the section on the computer industry are Engil Juliussen and Karen Petska-Juliussen, *Computer Industry Almanac: 1994-1995*, The Reference Press, Inc., 1994; and Jacqueline Warnke, "Computer manufacturing: change and competition," *Monthly Labor Review*, August 1996, pp. 18-29.

[4] The comparisons here are between the "Computer and office equipment" industry (Code 357 of the Standard Industrial Classification {"SIC"}) and the "Motor vehicles and equipment" industry (SIC code 371). See *Statistical Abstract of the United States*, 1989, pp. 720-723; and *Statistical Abstract of the United States*, 1996, pp. 733-737.

[5] The comparison is with 1976. See *Statistical Abstract of the United States*, 1979, pp. 806-811.

[6] This is according to BLS projections. See James C. Franklin, "Industry output and employment projections to 2005," *Monthly Labor Review,* November 1995, p. 53.

[7] See *Statistical Abstract of the United States*, 1990, p. 784; and *Statistical Abstract of the United States*, 1996, p. 776.

[8] See *Statistical Abstract of the United States*, 1989, p. 410; and *Statistical Abstract of the United States*, 1996, p. 419. See also Laura Freeman, "Job creation and the emerging home computer market," *Monthly Labor Review*, August 1996, pp. 46-56.

[9] See Karen Friefeld, "Computers—surging sales; Computer companies

gear up for a competitive holiday season as more and more consumers look to buy a home PC," *Newsday*, October 8, 1995, p. 1.

[10] See *Statistical Abstract of the United States*, 1996, p. 421; and Freeman, p. 47.

[11] See William C. Goodman, "The software and engineering industries: threatened by technological change?" *Monthly Labor Review*, August 1996, p. 37.

[12] See Goodman, pp. 40-41.

[13] See *World Data 1995*, World Bank Indicators on CD-ROM, 1995; and *Statistical Abstract of the United States*, 1996, pp. 796, 805.

[14] See *Statistical Abstract of the United States*, 1979, p. 803; and *Statistical Abstract of the United States*, 1996, p. 746.

[15] See Lauren A. Murray, "Unraveling employment trends in textiles and apparel," *Monthly Labor Review*, August 1995, p. 63; and "Current Labor Statistics," *Monthly Labor Review*, August 1996, p. 84.

[16] See Peter Morici, "Export our way to prosperity," *Foreign Policy*, Winter 1995-96, p. 3 [http://www.enews.com/magazines/foreign_policy/archives/120194.1.html February 10, 1997].

[17] See *Statistical Abstract of the United States*, 1996, pp. 784-785, for 1987-1995. Data for 1996 are estimated by Hudson Institute by extrapolation.

[18] Imports of capital goods, excluding automobiles, amounted to $222 billion in 1995. That was 30 percent of all imports and 138 percent of consumer goods imports (excluding automobiles). See Christopher L. Bach, "U.S. International Transactions, Fourth Quarter and Year 1995," *Survey of Current Business*, April 1996, p. 52.

[19] See *Workers in an Integrating World*, World Bank, World Development Report 1995, pp. 164-165 and 186-187.

[20] See, for example, Paul Krugman, "The myth of Asia's miracle," *Foreign Affairs*, Nov/Dec 1994, pp. 62-78.

[21] The most important of these include guarantees of basic property rights, well-run legal systems, and limited, uncorrupt bureaucracies. See *The Economist*, March 1, 1997, pp. 71-72.

[22] It is also true that the Asian developing countries need to continue to liberalize their economies if they are to continue to grow rapidly. On this, see "Asia's precarious miracle," *The Economist*, March 1, 1997, p. 18.

[23] *Workers in an Integrating World*, p. 222.

[24] *Workers in an Integrating World*, p. 166.

[25] See *Workers in an Integrating World*, pp. 186-187.

[26] See *From Plan to Market*, World Bank, World Development Report 1996.

27 See *Statistical Abstract of the United States*, 1996, p. 21.

28 Paul Krugman, *Pop Internationalism*, MIT Press, 1996, p. 211.

29 See *Historical Statistics of the United States, 1789-1945*, Bureau of the Census, 1949, pp. 63-65. See also *Statistical Abstract of the United States*, 1995, CD-ROM version, Table 668.

30 Bureau of Economic Analysis, *Regional Projections to 2045*; Volume 1, July 1995. The projections were prepared by the Industry and Projections Branch, a part of BEA's Regional Economic Analysis Division.

31 Data are from Bureau of Labor Statistics industry-occupation matrices contained in files Pub8386.dbf, Pub8788.dbf, Pub8990.dbf, and Pub9193.dbf, downloaded June 30, 1996. See also Neal H. Rosenthal, "The nature of occupational employment growth: 1983-93," *Monthly Labor Review*, June 1995, pp. 45-54.

32 See Chapter 2, Tables 2-4 and 2-5 below. See also George T. Silvestri, "Occupational employment to 2005," *Monthly Labor Review*, November 1995, pp. 60-84.

33 See "Warp speed," *Economist*, October 26, 1996 [http://www.enews.com/magazines/economist/archive/1996/10/961026-009.html February 24, 1997].

CHAPTER TWO

1 Data are from Diana Furchtgott-Roth's *Women's Figures*, a study released by the Independent Women's Forum and quoted in Christopher Caldwell, "The Feminization of America," *Weekly Standard*, December 23, 1996, p. 18.

2 These data include married-couple families with at least one income earner. *Statistical Abstract of the United States*, 1996, p, 427.

3 The comparisons are of persons 20 years of age and older. See *Report on the American Workforce*, U.S. Department of Labor, 1995, pp. 146-147; and *Statistical Abstract of the United States*, 1996, p. 393.

4 See *Statistical Abstract of the United States*, 1996, p. 400. Women are more than proportionately numbered among part-time workers, and undoubtedly many of these are women with young children.

5 Employers are, of course, already beginning to offer such benefits. Thus human-resource executives from IBM, AT&T, Johnson & Johnson, Xerox, Exxon, and other major corporations have formed the American Business Collaboration for Quality Dependent Care — a $100-million consortium to finance improvements in community child-care and elder-care services in their regions of operation. See the report in the *Wall Street Journal*, January 15, 1997, p. B1.

6 See, e.g., "The Downsizing of America," a seven-part series appearing in the *New York Times*, March 3-9, 1996; and Donald L. Barlett and James B.

Steele, "America: who stole the dream?" a ten-part series appearing in the *Philadelphia Inquirer*, September 9-22, 1996.

[7] See, e.g., the statement of then-Senator Howard Metzenbaum (D-OH) at the "Conference on the growing contingent workforce: Flexibility at the price of fairness?: Conference before the Subcommittee on Labor of the Senate Committee on Human Resources," 103d Congress, 2d Session (1994).

[8] Job tenure is measured by the median number of years workers aged 25 and older have had the same employer.

[9] "Employee tenure in the mid-1990s," Bureau of Labor Statistics, January 30, 1997 [ftp://stats.bls.gov/pub/news.release/tenure.txt].

[10] See *Report on the American Workforce*, pp. 12-13.

[11] See *Report on the American Workforce*, p. 25.

[12] See Anne E. Polivka, "A profile of contingent workers," *Monthly Labor Review*, October 1996, pp. 10-21.

[13] *Report on the American Workforce*, pp. 28-31.

[14] See, e.g., "Hired out: Workers are forced to take more jobs with few benefits," *Wall Street Journal*, March 11, 1993, p. A1; and Jeremy Rifkin, *The End of Work*, G. P. Putnam's Sons, 1995, pp. 190-191.

[15] *Report on the American Workforce*, U.S. Department of Labor, 1995, p. 38.

[16] The increase may be as great as 25 percent annually, if we believe the data attributed to the National Association of Temporary and Staffing Services (NATSS) in the *Wall Street Journal*, February 18, 1997, p. B1. On the other hand, the NATSS reported that American companies paid only $4.6 billion for temporary help in 1995. That sum is minuscule compared to the nation's total wage bill of $3.4 *trillion*. See *Statistical Abstract of the United States*, 1995, p. 451.

[17] That claim is made by NATSS, as reported in the *Wall Street Journal*, February 18, 1997, p. B1.

[18] "Temporary help services continue growth; Several factors cited," National Association of Temporary and Staffing Services [http://www.podi.com/staffing/anupda.txt February 19, 1997].

[19] "Temporary jobs: Making them work for you," downloaded to Hudson Institute from NATSS website, http://www.natss.com/staffing/making.txt. According to the NATSS profile of temporary workers, 38 percent of those offered full-time employment declined it, because they preferred their "contingent" status. Nearly 40 percent declared that they would prefer to work "permanently as temporaries."

[20] U.S. Department of Transportation, *Transportation Implications of Telecommuting*, April 1993.

[21] Jack Nilles, JALA International, Inc., "Telecommuting forecasts," Los Angeles, CA, 1991.

[22] Link Resources Corporation of New York, as cited in Mark Hecquet, "How telecommuting transforms work," *Training*, November 1994, p. 56.

[23] Gail Dutton, "Can California change its corporate culture?" *Management Review*, June 1994, p. 49.

[24] Congressional Office of Technology Assessment, *The Technological Reshaping of Metropolitan America*, September 1995. "Mobile activities" include those such as traveling sales work, management consulting, and auditing.

[25] *Statistical Abstract of the United States*, 1996, pp. 405-407; and George T. Silvestri, "Occupational employment to 2005," *Monthly Labor Review*, November 1995, p. 61.

[26] The index is computed first by weighting the number of workers in each occupation by its average weekly wage in one particular year (in this case, 1993) and then summing across all major occupational categories. The number so computed is then compared to the equivalent figure for a base year (in this case, 1983). The index measures the change in the earning power of the American workforce *due only to its occupational composition*; it is completely uninfluenced by changing levels of compensation. Symbolically, the Index of Job Quality is expressed as follows:

Let:

w_i^j = the average weekly earnings in the ith major occupational category (i.e., "Professional speciality;" "Service occupations;" "Technicians and related support;" etc. there are nine of these) in the jth year (where j = 1983, 1984, 1984…).

n_i^j = the number of employees in the ith major occupational category in the jth year.

Then I_j , the Index of Job Quality in the jth year, is defined as:

$$I_j = \frac{\sum_{i=1..9} w_i^{1993} n_i^j}{\sum_{i=1...9} w_i^{1993} n_i^{1983}}$$

[27] For example, between 1983 and 1994, the median weekly earnings of full-time "professional specialty workers" rose 3.3 times faster than those of "service workers." *Statistical Abstract of the United States*, 1986, p. 419; *Statistical Abstract of the United States*, 1996, p. 426

[28] See Maury Gittleman and Mary Joyce, "Earnings mobility in the United States," *Monthly Labor Review*, September 1995, p. 4.

[29] See W. Michael Cox and Richard Alm, "By our own bootstraps: Economic opportunity and the dynamics of income distribution," *Federal Reserve Bank of Dallas Annual Report*, 1995.

30 Cox and Alm, pp. 6, 8.

31 Cox and Alm, p. 12.

32 The analysis here is based on median annual earnings of full-time wage and salary workers aged 25 and older. Fringe benefits and other forms of non-wage and salary compensation are not included. The source of the data is U.S Bureau of the Census, *Current Population Reports*, Series P20-476, "Educational attainment in the United States: March 1993 and 1992," table 19 and [http://www.bls.gov/population/socdemo/education/table19.txt].

33 Includes year-round, full-time workers aged 15 years and older. U.S. Bureau of the Census, Historical Income Tables-Persons, Table 13 [http://www.census.gob.ftp/pub/hhes/income/histinc/p13.html].

34 *Statistical Abstract of the United States*, 1996, p. 52.

35 There is great heterogeneity within the U.S. Hispanic population with respect to education. BLS data indicate that the 53.4 percent of all Hispanics aged 25 years and older in 1995 possessed at least a high school education. *Within* the Hispanic population, however, the analogous figure for Mexicans was 46.5 percent, whereas for all other Hispanics (Puerto Ricans, Cubans, etc.) the figure was above 60 percent. See *Statistical Abstract of the United States*, 1996, p. 51.

36 George Vernez and Allan Abrahamse, "How immigrants fare in U.S. education," RAND Corporation, 1996 [http//www/rand.org./publications/MR/MR718/].

37 See Gary Steinberg, "The class of '90 one year after graduation," *Occupational Outlook Quarterly*, Summer 1994. See also John Tsapogas, *Characteristics of Recent Science and Engineering Graduates: 1990*, National Science Foundation report 92-316, 1992.

38 See Silvestri, pp. 60-87. The "moderate" estimate is based on a projected annual rate of 2.3 percent growth in GDP. See Norman C. Saunders, "The U.S. economy to 2005," *Monthly Labor Review*, November 1995, pp. 10-28.

39 The database underlying this analysis incorporates the *Dictionary of Occupational Titles*, Fourth Edition, Revised 1991 (DOT); the 1992 version of *Occupational Employment Statistics* (OES), a survey of occupations and their relationship to the DOT as defined by the BLS; and BLS file OPTDDATA.DATA downloaded to Hudson Institute on August 30, 1996, containing data appearing in *Occupational Projections and Training Data*, 1996 edition BLS Bulletin 2471, January 1996. The employment projections are discussed in Silvestri.

40 We reach this conclusion by looking at job openings in the following occupational categories: agriculture, forestry, fishing, and related fields (988,000); precision production, craft, and repair (4,489,000); operators, fabricators, and laborers (5,626,000); marketing and sales (6,706,000—many of which are relatively low-skilled sales positions); and administrative support

(6,991,000). Adding the totals in each of these categories yields 24.8 million jobs—exactly half of the 49.6 million jobs projected to open between 1994 and 2005, according to the BLS.

[41] We may arbitrarily date that first sighting as in 1987, the year in which *Workforce 2000* was published.

[42] *Economic Report of the President*, 1997, p. 338.

[43] See "Job creation and employment opportunities: The United States labor market, 1993-1996," Council of Economic Advisers, April 23, 1996 [http://www.whitehouse.gov/WH/EOP/CEA/html/labor.html#conclusion January 3, 1997]. See also "Why more looks like less," *The Economist*, April 27, 1996 [http://www.enews.com/magazines/economist/archive/1996/04/960427-005.html January 3, 1997].

[44] Note, though, that recent projections from the same source (the Bureau of Labor Statistics) have underestimated the growth of the managerial and professional occupations while overestimating the growth of positions for poorly paid service workers. For example, in 1988 the BLS projected employment in the managerial occupations to increase by 29 percent between 1986 and 2000. In fact, by 1995 the number of workers in these occupations had already increased by 62 percent. The analogous numbers for projection and actual employment in the professional occupations were 27 percent and 34 percent, respectively. On the other hand, the growth in service workers from 1986 to 1995 was far below the BLS projection. In other words, if past tendencies hold, the BLS' current figures may well err by understating the good news and overstating the bad news. See *Projections 2000*, BLS Bulletin 2302, March 1988, p. 4; and *Statistical Abstract of the United States*, 1997, pp. 405-407.

[45] Only occupations with at least 100,000 workers in 1994 are listed. For more information, see Silvestri.

[46] The eight occupations are those of systems analysts; computer engineers; other computer scientists; teachers in special education; securities and financial-services sales workers; management analysts; instructors and coaches in sports and physical training; and food-service and lodging managers.

[47] The nine occupations are those of personal and home care aides; home health aides; physical therapists; medical assistants; other health-service workers; dental hygienists; dental assistants; and emergency medical technicians. Together these occupations will account for approximately 1.1 million additional jobs.

[48] On this point, see Frank Levy and Richard J. Murnane, "U.S. earnings levels and earnings inequality: A review of recent and proposed evaluations," *Journal of Economic Literature*, September 1992, pp. 1349, 1367, 1373.

[49] The database underlying this analysis incorporates the sources listed in note 32.

[50] *Workforce 2000*, Hudson Institute, 1987, p. 99.

CHAPTER THREE

[1] Most of the differences among the various Census Bureau projections come from different assumptions about immigration levels—not life spans or fertility rates. The Bureau's low projection for annual net immigration is 350,000, but the figures rise to 820,000 in the middle projection and 1,370,000 in the high one. See *Statistical Abstract of the United States,* 1996, p. 9.

[2] See Michael Fix and Jeffrey S. Passell, *Immigration and Immigrants: Setting the Record Straight,* Urban Institute, 1994, p. 40.

[3] Paul R. Campbell, "Population projections for states by age, sex, race, and Hispanic origin: 1995 to 2025," U.S. Bureau of the Census, October 1996 [http://www.census.gov/population/projections/state/stpjpop.txt March 12, 1997].

[4] *Economic Report of the President,* February 1997, pp. 99-101.

[5] The "surprise free" projection for 2020 relies heavily on the BLS 1994-2005 projection. It assumes that recent trends in labor-force growth will continue. It also assumes that BLS projections of labor-force participation rates to 2005 will remain valid and unchanged through 2020.

[6] Note that both Hudson projections of the size of the 2020 workforce assume that the annual number of net immigrants will hold constant at 820,000 until 2020.

[7] See George J. Borjas, Richard B. Freeman, and Lawrence F. Katz, "Searching for the effect of immigration on the labor market," *American Economic Review,* May 1996, p. 246.

[8] See Howard N. Fullerton Jr., "The 2005 labor force: growing, but slowly," *Monthly Labor Review,* November 1995, p. 34.

[9] Under these assumptions, the male participation rate for the 54-to-64-year-old group would return to its 1970 levels, and for 65-to-70-year-olds it would more than double to about 50 percent. For all other age groups, male participation rates would remain essentially unchanged. The assumptions for women are that participation rates for age groups 35-54 would achieve parity with male rates and those for 55-to-64-year-olds and 65-to-74-year-olds would rise to about 75 percent and 38 percent, respectively. These assumptions represent very large jumps in labor-force participation rates for both sexes, and they are made to highlight how sensitive labor-force growth is to significant changes in these participation rates.

[10] The Census Bureau sees the white non-Hispanic share of the population dropping to 52.8 percent by 2050. By then Hispanics are slated to comprise nearly a quarter of the population: the proportion of blacks will hold steady at 13-14 percent, and the proportion of Asians will rise above 8 percent.

[11] In keeping with U.S. government convention, the Census Bureau classifies Asians together with Pacific Islanders, but most Asian-Americans are of Chinese, Filipino, Japanese, Indian, or Indochinese extraction.

[12] *Workforce 2000*, p. 89.

[13] Recall, though, that persons with similar amounts of education—measured by years of schooling or degrees earned —can have very different earnings. The variation appears to be explained mainly by the different fields in which students concentrate and by the divergent quality of educational institutions.

[14] See Fix and Passell, pp. 33-35.

[15] *International Assessment of Educational Progress*. National Center for Education Statistics, U.S. Department of Education, 1992.

[16] In 1994 the graduation rate for whites was 82.6 percent; for blacks, 77 percent; and for Hispanics, 56.6 percent. The annual rate of change was a 0.005-percentage-point decline for whites; a 0.495-percentage-point gain for blacks; and a 0.035-percentage-point gain for Hispanics. For high school graduation rates, college attendance rates, and statistics on choice of degree, see *Fourteenth Annual Status Report on Minorities in Higher Education*, American Council on Education, 1996.

[17] In 1995 average composite SAT scores were 946 for whites, 744 for blacks, 802 for Mexican-Americans, 856 for Asians, and 850 for Native Americans. See *National Report: College-Bound Seniors, 1972-1995*, College Entrance Examination Board, 1996. SAT scores were "recentered" in 1996, which means that 1996 scores cannot be compared with those from earlier years.

[18] Statistics on time needed to earn a degree are from the 1994 and 1996 editions of *Condition of Education*, U.S. Department of Education, 1996.

CHAPTER FOUR

[1] One estimate is that increasing the share of trade in Gross Domestic Product by one percentage point raises income per person by 2 percent or more. See Jeffrey Frankel and David Romer, "Trade and Growth: An Empirical Investigation," National Bureau of Economic Research Working Paper 5476, 1996. A smaller but quite significant impact is also found in Robert Barro and Xavier Sala-i-Martin, *Economic Growth*, McGraw Hill, 1995. Studies by the World Bank and the Organization for Economic Cooperation and Development have come to the same conclusion: free trade increases wealth.

[2] Orley Ashenfelter et al., "Employment Performance," McKinsey Global Institute, November 1994.

[3] New methods of counting the labor force added approximately 1.1 million to the measurement in 1994 and later years. This had the effect of making labor force participation rates appear to be 0.3 percent higher, compared with previous data. Figures for 1994 and later have therefore been adjusted downward by 1.1 million, to make them more comparable to the figures for previous years. See "New Measures of the Work Force," Federal Reserve Bank of San

Francisco *Weekly Letter*, March 18, 1994. See also *Economic Report of the President*, 1996, footnote 5 to Table B-31, p. 307.

[4] Some argue that U.S. productivity growth has been understated by half a percentage point or so, but that would have been true in previous years as well. Thus the slowdown would still exist. There is little doubt that productivity gains have been understated in finance and other services, but productivity gains in manufacturing have been correspondingly exaggerated. If a manufacturer outsources services that used to be performed within the firm (e.g., accounting or law), the company appears to have the same output with fewer employees; but in fact, productivity has not increased.

[5] "Corporate Work At Home: The Office of the Future," *Ameritech*, January 1993.

[6] Lawrence Mishel and Ruy A. Teixeira, *The Myth of the Coming Labor Shortage*, Economic Policy Institute, 1991, p. 28. For a critique of a related publication from the same source, see "Working harder for less?" *The Economist*, September 7, 1996.

[7] George Borjas, Richard Freeman, and Lawrence Katz, "On the labor market effects of immigration and trade," National Bureau of Economic Research Working Paper 3761, 1990.

[8] Sol Stern, "Back to Work," the *Wall Street Journal*, September 7, 1993, p.A14.

[9] John Hood, "The market approach to job training," *Policy Review*, May-June 1996.

[10]Chester E. Finn Jr., Bruno V. Manno, and Louann Bierlein, *Charter Schools in Action: What Have We Learned?*, Hudson Institute, 1996.

INDEX

ABOUT THE AUTHORS

Richard W. Judy is a Senior Research Fellow at Hudson Institute. Mr. Judy specializes in issues concerning domestic and international economic development. His previous work at Hudson includes project directorships for studies of economic reform and development in Hungary, the Baltic states, Russia, and Ukraine. He headed Hudson's program to develop indigenous economic policy research institutes ("think tanks") in formerly socialist countries.

Mr. Judy studied economics and computer science at the University of Kansas, Columbia University, and Harvard University. Before coming to Hudson he was Professor of Economics and Computer Science at the University of Toronto. He also has been the founder and CEO of two successful high-tech companies. His most recent book was *The Information Age and Soviet Society,* of which he was co-author. His writings have appeared in such forums as the *Wall Street Journal, Washington Times, National Review, International Executive,* and the *Wall Street Journal Europe.*

Carol D'Amico is a Senior Research Fellow and Director of the *Workforce 2020* project. Since joining Hudson in 1990, she has developed several comprehensive programs designed to restructure public schools. Before joining Hudson, Dr. D'Amico was a Policy and Planning Specialist for the Indiana Superintendent of Public Instruction, focusing on strategies to improve public education. She also served as Senior Program Analyst for the Indiana General Assembly, where she analyzed state government policies and operations.

Dr. D'Amico holds an Ed.D. in leadership and policy studies from Indiana University, where she also earned an M.S. in adult education. She has been cited in numerous publications including the *Indianapolis Star, Indianapolis Business Journal, Business Week,* and *Education Week* and comments frequently on education issues for local and national television and radio programs. She has testified to Congress and several state legislatures on job training and education issues.

ABOUT HUDSON INSTITUTE

Hudson Institute is a private, not-for-profit research organization founded in 1961 by the late Herman Kahn. Hudson analyzes and makes recommendations about public policy for business and government executives, as well as for the public at large. The institute does not advocate an express ideology or political position. However, more than thirty years of work on the most important issues of the day has forged a viewpoint that embodies skepticism about the conventional wisdom, optimism about solving problems, a commitment to free institutions and individual responsibility, an appreciation of the crucial role of technology in achieving progress, and an abiding respect for the importance of values, culture, and religion in human affairs.

Since 1984, Hudson has been headquartered in Indianapolis, Indiana. It also maintains offices in Washington, D.C.; Madison, Wisconsin; San Antonio, Texas; and Montreal, Canada.